Real Estate Tax Secrets of the Rich

Big-Time Tax Advantages of Buying, Selling, and Owning Real Estate

Sandy Botkin, CPA, Esq.

McGraw-Hill

New York   Chicago   San Francisco   Lisbon   London
Madrid   Mexico City   Milan   New Delhi   San Juan
Seoul   Singapore   Sydney   Toronto

This publication is designed to provide accurate and authoritative information in regard to the subject matter covered. It is sold with the understanding that neither the author nor the publisher is engaged in rendering legal, accounting, or other professional service. If legal advice or other expert assistance is required, the services of a competent professional person should be sought.

—From a Declaration of Principles jointly
adopted by Committee of the American Bar
Association and a Committee of Publishers.

McGraw-Hill books are available at special quantity discounts to use as premiums and sales promotions, or for use in corporate training programs. For more information, please write to the Director of Special Sales, McGraw-Hill Professional, Two Penn Plaza, New York, NY 10121-2298. Or contact your local bookstore.

Contents

Dedications and Acknowledgments   vii

Introduction   ix

Part 1 Overview of Real Estate   *1*

Chapter 1. Why You Should Own Your Home   3

Chapter 2. Buy a Home or Die in Poverty   11

Part 2 Tax Goodies from Owning a Home   *17*

Chapter 3. Tax Basis—The Starting Place
for All Deductions   19

Chapter 4. IRS Record-Keeping Requirements to
Bulletproof Your Basis   25

Chapter 5. Why Making Improvements to Your
Home Is Much More Valuable than Making Repairs   31

Chapter 6. Maximizing the New Mortgage Interest Rules   37

Chapter 7. The Point of Points   45

Chapter 8. Maximizing Your Deductions when
Building a Home   51

Chapter 9. Maximizing the Effect of Real Estate Taxes   55

Contents

Part 3 Maximizing Tax Benefits when You Dispose of Your Home   **59**

Chapter 10. Excluding Gain when You Sell Your Home—An Overview of the New Universal Exclusion   **61**

Chapter 11. Exceptions to the Two-Year Rule   **67**

Chapter 12. Divorce and Death Implications   **71**

Chapter 13. Using an S Corporation to Avoid the Two-Year Rule   **77**

Part 4 Introduction to Tax Planning for Buying and Looking for Rental Property   **83**

Chapter 14. Introduction to Investment Property   **85**

Chapter 15. Understanding Depreciation   **89**

Chapter 16. How to Evaluate Rates of Return for Residential Investment Property   **95**

Chapter 17. How to Deduct the Cost of Looking for Property   **101**

Part 5 Tax Goodies Incurred while Owning Rental Property   **107**

Chapter 18. Minimizing Passive Loss Problems   **109**

Chapter 19. Maximizing Your Depreciation Deductions   **121**

Chapter 20. Making Land Deductible   **127**

Chapter 21. Splitting Income by Hiring Family Members   **135**

Chapter 22. Why Repairs on Investment Property Are Important   **141**

Part 6 Minimizing Taxes when Disposing of Real Estate   **151**

Chapter 23. How to Calculate Gain or Loss   **153**

Chapter 24. When to Use Seller Financing   **155**

Chapter 25. How to Avoid All Gain on the Sale of Investment Property Using Like-Kind Exchanges   **171**

Chapter 26. Sales to Relatives   **181**

Part 7 Miscellaneous Real Estate Tax Considerations   *185*

Chapter 27. Understanding Vacation Home and Second Home Rules   **187**

Chapter 28. Tax Benefits of Owning Motels, Hotels, and Bed-and-Breakfasts   **195**

Chapter 29. Frequently Asked Questions   **201**

Appendix 1 Recommended Tax Resources   **209**

Appendix 2 Leveraging Today's Technology   **213**

Appendix 3 Forms   **219**

Index   **222**

Dedications and Acknowledgments

I dedicate this book to my wife, Lori, and my children, Jeremy, Matthew, and Allison, for their endless patience and sense of wonder and playfulness, and to my students, who helped craft this work with feedback and suggestions. I thank Jim Piccalo for letting me test my programs with his real estate school, and I thank Pat Quinlin, my personal editor, who significantly helped in the edits of the manuscript. I also thank Sally Glover and Mary Glenn, my editors at McGraw-Hill, for their input and timely suggestions.

There were numerous other folks who provided suggestions for this book. I thank Howard Kaplan, attorney at law in Omaha, Nebraska; Debbie Spoons of Tax Sentinel I; The Manhattan Tax Club; and Mike Sampson, Professor of Taxation at American University, for their reviews of this book.

I also want to specifically thank Allison Botkin for her timely edits of all cartoons and illustrations contained in this book.

Finally, I want to dedicate this book to the U.S. Congress, which makes this work not only possible, but necessary.

Introduction

Historically, real estate has been one of the greatest tax shelters in the United States. A solid knowledge of real estate taxation can increase most people's rate of return on their homes and investment property by 10 percent to 20 percent per year—no kidding! During years when real estate doesn't appreciate (which happens in all areas), tax benefits may be your only return on investment.

Sadly, many terrific tax-planning techniques that the wealthy have been using for years are not known by most people. Most real estate books currently on the market don't have this information.

Now you'll learn what the rich have been doing for decades regarding real estate. All strategies are footnoted to the Internal Revenue Code (IRC), IRS Regulations (REGS), IRS rulings, and case law. Your accountant can check out everything quickly for validity. This book is based on my course, "Wealth-Building Real Estate Tax Strategies," which I have been presenting nationwide for many years and is available on my Web site: www.taxreductioninstitute.com.

Myths

After reading this book, you may wonder why you weren't aware of this information years ago. There are several myths that cause overpayment of taxes and lost deductions.

Myth 1: My accountant takes care of my taxes/my spouse takes care of our taxes. These seven words impoverish more people than any other myth. It's like saying "My doctor takes care of my body." Wouldn't it be great if we never had to exercise, could eat all the fattening foods we wanted, and once a year go to our doctor for a Roto-Rooter job? The point is that the tax savings your accountant can find for you are small compared to what you can save if you are pursuing your own tax strategies. If you don't know what to tell your accountant and don't have the tax strategies in place, you will lose thousands of dollars in deductions and write-offs.

Myth 2: I didn't make a lot of money this year, so I don't need to know about tax planning. This is absolutely false. If you own investment property or a home, you have access to the last great tax shelters in this country: your own business and real estate. Interestingly, if your investment real estate creates a loss, you can usually use a portion or even all of that loss against any form of other income such as dividends, rents, wages, and gains if you plan correctly and meet certain tests.[1]

Example: Richard and Mary earned $80,000 in salary but had investment real estate that generated a $10,000 loss deduction. If they are considered active investors (which I will describe later in this book), they may use this $10,000 loss against their $80,000 salary, giving them a net taxable income of $70,000.

Much of what makes real estate a good tax shelter is depreciation of buildings and equipment, which is a noncash deduction. Thus, you get a deduction without spending cash—pretty neat. Your mortgage payment might be $2,000 per month, but the depreciation on the property might be $4,000 per month. This is one reason why many wealthy people own investment property and use proper tax planning.

Myth 3: Tax knowledge won't save me much money anyway. The number-one expense for many Americans is taxes. It exceeds what most people pay for food, lodging, clothing, and transportation combined.[2] In two great books,[3] *Money Mastery* and *The Millionaire Next Door*, the authors analyze the mind-set of multimillionaires in order to determine what makes them tick. They found a number of interesting correlations.

First, most millionaires are frugal and live beneath their means. Sam Walton, for example, drove a pickup truck.

---

[1] Sections 469 (c),(d),(g),(i) of the IRC and Sections 1211(b) and 1231 of the IRC.

[2] *The Tax Foundation* and *The Tax Advisor* (American Institute of Certified Public Accountants), May 2000.

[3] *Money Mastery, 10 Principles That Will Change Your Financial Life Forever* by Williams, Jeppson, and Botkin (published by Career Press), and *The Millionaire Next Door: The Surprising Secrets of Americans Wealthy* by Thomas J. Stanley and William D. Danko (Longstreet Press 1996)

Second, most millionaires believe that if you want to get rich, you must get your taxes down to the legal minimum. They know that the best way to reduce taxes is to have your own business and to own both investment real estate and your home.

At the Success 2000 seminar, Donald Trump noted "If you want to get rich, you need to lower your taxes to the legal minimum." The rich understand that tax planning potentially leads to tremendous wealth.

Tax knowledge is very lucrative. The time it takes to read this book probably will put more money in your pocket than you could earn in that same time frame—and these savings will continue year after year.

What This Book Covers

A wide array of tax topics are covered in this book. You probably will find the answer to any real estate tax question that you have had or will have. Due to the scope of this subject, the book is divided into seven parts:

Part 1—Overview of Real Estate explains why it is essential to own your home. Some columnists expect the prices to fall in real estate. Are they right? You will be able to form your own conclusion because we will discuss the impact of various economic effects on real estate values. If you decide to buy a home instead of renting, you will also learn how much your payments should be in order to have the same net after-tax standard of living as you had while renting.

Part 2—Tax Goodies from Owning a Home is an in-depth discussion of the tax benefits of home ownership. Many of my students are surprised at how tax planning for home ownership can result in a dramatic reduction in taxes. We discuss important concepts such as basis, IRS required documentation, why it's essential to have improvements and what they are, how to plan for mortgage interest and taxes, how to plan for points, and tax planning when building a home. We explain the tax consequences of each item on the settlement sheet received when you close on your property, and this one aspect alone will pay for this book 100 times over!

Part 3—Maximizing Tax Benefits when You Dispose of Your Home deals with many important and little-known facts that can save you a bundle. We discuss the rules for the new Universal Exclusion, in which you can avoid up to $500,000 of gain, and show you how to do this over and over again on different properties. We explain the required rule that you must own the property and occupy it as your principal residence for two years. We delve into the numerous exceptions to the two-year rule. Remember, where there's a will … there's a lawyer. We reveal ways to find very motivated sellers by understanding tax consequences for divorces. You will learn how to avoid up to $500,000 of gain on rental properties. We explain how to get a step up in basis to current market value instead of using your original cost when you rent out your home.

Part 4—Introduction to Tax Planning for Buying and Looking for Rental Property starts our discussion of investment property. You will learn how to figure rates of return on residential investment property and how to deduct travel expenses when looking for real estate. You will learn how to classify and treat every item on the settlement statement you receive when you purchase investment property.

Part 5—Tax Goodies Incurred while Owning Rental Property deals with the basics of tax planning when you own investment property. This part shows how to use the loss from investment real estate against income on your tax return. We discuss how to figure depreciation and how to maximize its effects on your return. We explain something most realtors and accountants think is impossible: how to deduct the cost of the land that buildings are located on. We explain why repairs are so important in rental property, and we reveal concepts that the very wealthy have been using for years.

Part 6—Minimizing Taxes when Disposing of Real Estate deals with much of the tax planning that comes into play when you want to unload your investment property. We point out when you should use and when you should avoid seller financing. We discuss ways to avoid or defer all gains on the disposition of any investment property using a like-kind exchange. We uncover the traps you should be aware of when you sell your properties to relatives.

Part 7—Miscellaneous Real Estate Tax Considerations covers topics that don't fit into any of the above categories. We discuss various ways to take title and why using a limited liability company may make sense. Or should I say cents? We describe the tax aspects of owning second homes and vacation homes, and we answer some of the most common real estate questions I have been asked over the years.

There is also an appendix for you to find other materials and Web sites to give you more information on this subject.

Goals for Writing This Book

When I started writing this book, I had several goals in mind. First, I wanted to show readers (especially real estate owners, investors, real estate managers, and realtors) how to increase their rates of return on almost any property and how to save thousands of dollars on their taxes each year. I also wanted to present the material in a simplified format that was easy to understand. Plus, I wanted to emphasize little-known audit-proof documentation strategies needed to survive any IRS audit.

Practicality is the theme of this book, which includes hundreds of tips and suggestions that will save you a bundle each year. I wanted to show real estate professionals how to dramatically increase both their sales and listings by an understanding of basic real estate tax knowledge.

This book is the product of numerous lectures I have delivered to thousands of students over the years. In those lectures, I asked them to point out what was scary to them or what they didn't understand. My class, "Wealth Building Tax Secrets for Real Estate," is the result of this evolutionary process of many years of work.

I have provided all IRS annotations, which are the legal footnotes for everything that is discussed. Everything in this book is supported by appropriate documentation; thus, nothing I say should trigger an audit. Any questionable areas were omitted.

Throughout the book you will find icons that have the following meanings:

 Lightbulb—A tax-saving/money-making tip

Bomb—A cautionary tip or possible trap set up by Congress

Person with glasses—The author's elaboration or extra insight

Stack of money—Sales tip for realtors or tips that can provide more motivated sellers

I hope you get as much enjoyment from reading this book as I got from writing it!

Part 1

Overview of Real Estate

This part deals with real estate economics, what factors make real estate rise and fall, why you should own your home, and how you can afford it.

1

Why You Should Own Your Home

A fool and his money are soon parted. It takes creative tax laws for the rest.
—**Bob Thaves**

Tax laws can dramatically increase or decrease your investment return from both homes and rental properties. During years when real estate depreciation is stagnant, tax benefits may be the only return on investment you get. This book will alert you to the potential bottom-line returns resulting from this tax phenomenon.

Changes in tax laws can affect your investment return. Where possible, I will alert you to potential changes that will help you decide when to buy or sell and will help you in advising clients if you are a realtor, financial planner, or tax professional.

The book focuses on two types of properties:

- Homes—principal residences, second homes, and vacation homes
- Residential rental properties

Overview

1. Understand the four concepts in tax planning
2. Become aware of Uncle Sam's "gotchas," such as passive loss limits, phaseout of itemized deductions based on income, vacation home limits, and alternative minimum tax
3. Know how to avoid the myth "I can't afford the monthly payments if I buy instead of rent a home"
4. Learn how to compute the tax refund you would obtain as a result of owning a home and learn how to get this refund upfront monthly instead of waiting until after April 15

How Tax Law Helps You with Your Real Estate Investment

Think of Uncle Sam as a silent partner in your real estate investments—homes or rental property. You can use him to help finance your acquisition of homes and investment properties. In those situations, Uncle Sam becomes your banker. When you sell the property, he wants part of your profits and wants good documentation showing what these profits or losses are.

Four Concepts in Tax Planning

To reduce taxes, there are four different situations that cut Uncle Sam in as a financing partner. Everything discussed herein will involve one of these four strategies:

1. Tax exclusions: You use Uncle Sam to avoid tax altogether, such as with the Universal Exclusion on principal residences.
2. Tax deductions: You use Uncle Sam to help finance your payments for mortgage interest and real estate taxes for homes and other expenses for investment properties.

3. Tax deferral: You use Uncle Sam to postpone the tax on profits from disposing of property to help finance the acquisition for a buyer of your property. This will be utilized with seller carrybacks and like-kind exchanges.

4. Conversion: You use Uncle Sam to convert what would be ordinary income into tax-favored capital gain, which is taxed at a much lower rate.

Uncle Sam's "Gotchas" in Your Partnership Agreement

You want to maximize your tax partnership agreement with Uncle Sam, and this process is up to you. As long as you go along with tax law and have the appropriate documentation, you don't need any further agreement from him. Like any other partner, Uncle Sam wants his share of your profits, but he may not be willing to share in any future losses without careful planning. There are several limitations for using your tax goodies that might create tax traps if you don't watch out. As a brief overview, let's look at these "antigoody" provisions, which will be discussed in more detail later on.

Passive losses: Tax law classifies rental losses as passive losses that may or may not produce tax benefits on your tax return.[1] For now, keep in mind that a rental loss might not produce the desired current year losses on your return. Details of passive loss limitations are discussed in Chapter 18.

Vacation home limitations: This nasty provision is designed to curb tax benefits for your second home and when you rent out your main home or rent out a room in your main home. Details of these provisions are discussed in Chapter 27.

Alternative Minimum Tax: To make some people's life really ugly, Congress enacted the Alternative Minimum Tax (AMT).[2] This is one of the least understood traps in tax law that applies to the deductions involving principal residences and second homes. It is a parallel tax to income tax to ensure that everyone pays some taxes. Unfortunately, many taxpayers get caught in its tentacles by mistake and are unaware of its perils. I will look at the outlines of AMT here and pinpoint the specific traps where appropriate throughout the book.

Essentially, a number of people need to make two separate tax calculations. You have one set of rules for normal income tax and another set for AMT; you pay to the government whichever produces the higher amount.

To compute your AMT, take your regular taxable income and adjust it in three ways (some of the details of these adjustments will be discussed in later sections):

1. Remove some of your regular tax deductions such as home equity debt interest, state taxes, and local taxes. (Yes, you read correctly.)
2. Add so-called "tax preferences" not taxed under regular tax such as tax-exempt interest on some private-purpose municipal bonds.
3. Make timing adjustments that either accelerate income or delay deductions, such as reducing the amount of depreciations in a year and spreading it out over a longer period.

You reduce the resulting amount (called alternative minimum taxable income or AMT) by the alternative minimum taxable exemption, which depends on your filing status. If this isn't fun enough, the exemptions start phasing out above specified income levels.

You then apply a flat 26 percent rate up to the first $175,000 and 28 percent to everything above that, then pay the higher of your AMT tax or regular income tax.

Sandy's elaboration: You might ask, as I have: If Congress didn't want you to have the deductions, exclusions, and favorable timing of depreciation, why did it allow them to begin with? So much for tax simplification! As of this writing, there is a movement in Congress to either eliminate the AMT for individuals or increase its exemption. Although more people seem to be getting caught in AMT clutches, it is a small minority.

The three biggest items that catch people within its web are very high itemized deductions (such as gifts to charities), large amounts of qualified stock options, and large employee business expenses.

Generally, real estate losses are deductible for AMT. Large capital gains could present a problem.

How to Afford the Increased Monthly Payments When Buying a Home Instead of Renting:
Myth: I Can't Afford the Monthly Payments.

I am constantly shocked by how many people rent instead of buy their own homes. They believe that because buying requires a higher monthly payment, they can't afford it. This, in many cases, is a myth due to a misunderstanding of how the tax law affects us all.

When you buy a home or rental property, you get additional deductions that you would not have if you rented a place to live or invested in securities rather than real estate. These deductions could create a tax refund unless you plan for them up front. You can get that refund each month (instead of waiting until you file your tax return) by a change in your payroll withholding.

Sandy's tip: You do *not* want a tax refund. Overpayment of tax is an interest-free loan to the government. It is better to get the money up front each month.

$3,300 equals one dependent[3]: In general, tax deductions equal to $3,300 produce one withholding allowance, which is the allowance that you get for one child. For withholding purposes, $33,000 of new deductions for home mortgage interest, real estate taxes, and extra useable losses from rental properties is like giving birth to ten children ... but a lot less painful.

You can use IRS publication 919, *How Do I Adjust My Withholding?*, to see how the dollar amount you have withheld compares to your estimated annual tax. Call 1-800-TAX-FORM (1-800-829-3676) to get this publication. For more information, the IRS has an excellent Web site at www.irs.gov.

Let's examine how to compute withholding exemptions with an example. (Also see Figure 1-1.)

Example of how withholding allowances are computed[4]: Jim Nelson, a single taxpayer, earns $72,000 of net taxable income. He purchases his first home and wants to get money from Uncle Sam to help with his monthly mortgage. We are assuming that he incurs nine additional exemptions resulting from new mortgage interest and taxes totaling $28,000 per year.

Sandy's tip: What this means is that Nelson can now afford monthly payments of $1,973 and have the same standard of living and after-tax net cash that he had while he was renting. The point is that you do NOT want to wait until April 15 to get a tax refund. Use IRS Forms W-4 and IRS Publication 505 to reduce your interest-free loans to the government.

Watch out for itemized deduction reduction: As a result of some tax simplification (which means many folks got shafted by your kindly Uncle Sam), the value of your newfound home mortgage deductions for both interest and taxes will be reduced if your adjusted gross income is over $150,500 ($75,250 for married filing separately). This reduction is equal to 2 percent of your adjusted gross income in excess of these threshold amounts.[5] Thus, an adjusted gross income of $220,000 for a single person would reduce itemized deductions by $1,390. The good news is that this 2 percent reduction may not reduce itemized deductions below 80 percent

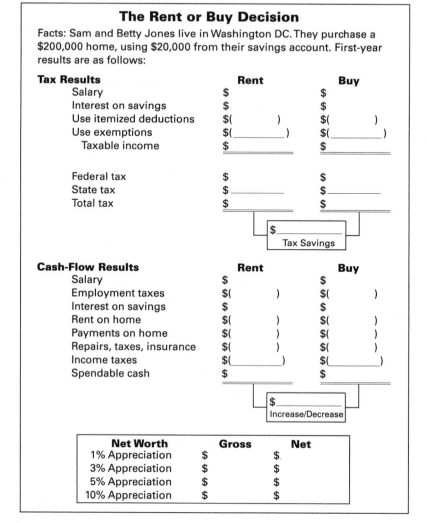

Figure 1-1

of the total amount claimed.[6] Also, you should note that medical expenses, investment interest expenses, and casualty and theft losses are not subject to this reduction.

If you pay estimated taxes in advance, through quarterly vouchers rather than through withholding, you may use the same tax deductions and credits in computing your estimated taxes.[7] Your goal should be to pay the least amount of tax in advance without penalty.

Step 1: How Nelson computes withholding allowances:

	Before	After
Personal allowances	1	1
Allowances from estimated deductions	0	9
Total	1	10

Step 2: How Nelson converts home purchase to instant cash:

Monthly federal income tax withheld	
With one withholding exemption	$1,226
With ten withholding exemptions	$453
Savings each month	$773
Months	12
Annual savings	$9,276

Step 3: How Nelson justified home purchase:

Rent he was paying	$1,200
Tax withholding benefit of new purchase	$773
Monthly cash available for home-purchase	$1,973

Summary

- There are four tax benefits that apply to real estate. You can exclude gain from being taxed with your principal residence. You can deduct mortgage interest and taxes on your principal residence and second home. You can defer gains to future years using installment sales and exchanges with rental property. You can convert what would be ordinary income into tax-favored long-term capital gain.
- You need to be aware of various tax traps that are discussed in this book, including passive loss limitations on your investment properties, alternative minimum tax, vacation home limits when you rent out a room or rent out your vacation home, and the possible elimination of some itemized deductions for mortgage interest and taxes if you make over a specified amount of money.
- Never get a tax refund if you can avoid it. If you are buying a home or investment property, use the increased deductions for mortgage interest, property taxes, or expected investment property losses to reduce your monthly withholding or estimated taxes. This way you will get your tax benefit up front each month.
- Remember, for every $3,300 of new real estate deductions or expected losses, you can add one exemption from withholding.

Notes

1 Section 469 of the Internal Revenue Code
2 Sections 53, and 55-59 of the IRC
3 Section 151 (d)(1)(A) of the IRC
4 IRS Publication 505 and IRS Form W-4
5 Section 68 of the IRC
6 Section 68 (a)(2) of the IRC
7 Section 6654 of the IRC

2

Buy a Home or Die in Poverty

I want to find out who this FICA guy is and how come he's taking so much of my money.
—Nick Kypreos, Former NHL Hockey Player

Chapter Overview
1. Learn why it is so important to buy your own home rather than lease or rent
2. Understand the basic principle of leverage as it applies to real estate
3. Learn how real estate has performed since 1998
4. Understand how fluctuation in interest rates affects real estate values
5. Understand how management fees affect real estate values
6. Learn why you should get rid of mortgage insurance whenever possible and understand a tax planning tip that should eliminate the need for mortgage insurance

The first real estate purchased by most Americans is a place to live, which should be purchased before you buy rental property—after all, you need a place to live. For most Americans, their homes make it possible to capture most of their net worth.

Everyone needs shelter; they can either rent and make landlords rich or they can buy their own homes and put that equity into their own pockets. Your purchase of a home will build your net worth. Paying rent is like throwing your money into the trash—there is no return on investment, and there is no equity buildup. To increase your net worth, you must own your home and investments that grow and build equity.

The problem is that money is a sneaky critter. It has a way of finding its way into another's pocket. It makes little difference how much or little you make, money tends to leak out of your pocket. This was amply shown in the book, *Money Mastery*, by Alan Williams et al., which I recommend

that you get. You need a trap for money. Home ownership is a perfect trap for money because each month you will be paying your mortgage and building up equity.

Leverage

Leverage means using other people's money. When prices rise, the ability to use borrowed funds (other people's money—OPM) multiplies the return. This is because the appreciation in the value of real estate belongs to the owner, regardless of who provided the money to buy it. Almost no investment equals the return you achieve when you stop paying rent, take out a mortgage, and buy a home that goes up in value.

Example of Leverage

Tom purchases a home for $300,000. He buys it using a $60,000 down payment and finances the rest. If the house appreciates by 5 percent, which means it appreciates by $15,000 (5 percent of $300,000—not 5 percent of the down payment), Tom makes a whopping 25 percent on his money ($15,000 appreciation/$60,000 down payment). If the house appreciates

10 percent or $30,000 he makes a whopping 50 percent on his money! Where else can you obtain this type of gain?

No other investment offers you a greater opportunity to use other people's money to help you build your net worth. Figure 2-1 shows how real estate has performed since 1998. You will notice that it has appreciated significantly each year. Historical rates of home appreciation for seven-year blocks of time have outpaced the consumer price index since World War II. Real estate has appreciated approximately 10 percent per year. No wonder most millionaires who are listed in the Forbes Richest Americans list have made their fortunes in real estate.

Real Estate Economics

You've probably heard some experts note that real estate is overpriced and is expected to level off. Others expect real estate to keep rising. How can we know what to expect? Although my crystal ball is being repaired, there are a number of factors that affect values and rates of return on real estate.

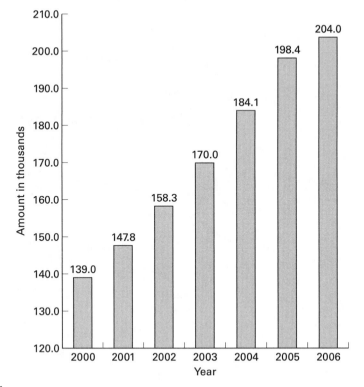

Figure 2-1

Interest Rates

Interest rate fluctuations have been shown to have a reverse correlation to real estate values. If interest rates start rising, prices tend to fall; when interest rates start falling or stay low, real estate prices tend to rise. I asked some accountants to analyze rates of return with differing assumptions. One analysis noted that a simple 1 percent drop in interest rates can increase profits by 26 percent. A drop from 10 percent to 8 percent in interest rates increases the annual compound after-tax profit by a whopping 46 percent. Shopping for the lowest interest rates is a smart idea.

 Hot tip: Due to the cost of refinancing and paperwork hassles, it generally doesn't profit to refinance unless there is at least a 1 percent point drop.

Management Fees

We did a projection on property that earned 10.58 percent annual after-tax profits even with paying a management fee of 8 percent. By eliminating the management fee, our profit zoomed to a 13.58 percent return on our investment, which is a 28 percent increase!

Sandy's elaboration: Find a way to eliminate management fees and you will increase your rate of return by almost 30 percent over what you would receive when paying the fees. Some methods of eliminating management fees are:

- Renting to a reliable relative
- Making sure you have a good tenant who can act as manager. An example of this involves some friends. They bought a town home near their son's college. The son takes care of the place and collects rent from other kids who are renting rooms.
- Using a shared-equity financing agreement to make the tenant a manager. This involves making the tenant a part-owner, whereby the tenant pays a share of the mortgage and pays you rent on your share of the ownership.
- Using lease-options to make the tenant want to keep the property in good shape. Many of my friends rent out property with an option for the tenant to buy the house. If the tenant exercises the option, the tenant will want to take good care of the property.

Unemployment

The higher unemployment is in an area, the more depressed real estate values become. Likewise, the better the job market, the more real estate values escalate.

Schools

People love sending their kids to top schools. Where I live, both our middle school and high school won national blue ribbons and were given state awards. Real estate values skyrocketed afterward. Top schools are always a big draw. Likewise, when school quality starts declining, real estate values follow suit.

Mortgage Insurance

A number of lenders make you buy mortgage insurance each year when your down payment does not meet a 20 percent minimum. With zero mortgage insurance, we can raise our rate of return approximately 5 percent.[1]

Sandy's tip: Getting rid of mortgage insurance is well worth it. Consider either putting up a down payment of at least 20 percent or use an owner take-back to keep the principal amount under the mortgage insurance requirements. The principal amount that you borrow should be less than

80 percent of the appraised value. If you already have enough equity in your home so that the equity exceeds 80 percent of the home's value, you should contact your lender to get the mortgage insurance dropped—usually they will.

Let's discuss why real estate has appreciated over the last few years in most parts of the country. We have had low interest rates that haven't changed much, and we have had low unemployment.

As of this writing, interest rates and unemployment are still low. I foresee, at least in the near future unless these factors change, increasing real estate values. However, watch out for increasing interest rates or unemployment rates. Should these change significantly, this will also affect real estate values.

Summary

- You should buy your own home before you buy investment property.
- Leverage is one of the reasons that real estate is such a great investment. Leverage means using other people's money.
- Rising interest rates mean dropping real estate values, while dropping interest rates usually mean rising real estate values.
- Eliminating management fees can result in a 28 percent increase in your rate of return for real estate.
- High unemployment means dropping real estate values in the area of unemployment.
- Good schools mean high real estate values.
- Get rid of mortgage insurance when your equity is at least 20 percent. It will increase your rate of return by 5 percent.

Notes

1 We originally had a 10.58 percent rate of return on a sample investment property. However, with the elimination of mortgage insurance, our rate of return went to 11.09 percent, which is a 5 percent increase.

Part 2

Tax Goodies from Owning a Home

This part discusses the fundamental concept of *basis*, which is used throughout the book. It also covers IRS record-keeping requirements for all real property. You will learn why making improvements to your home is much better than making repairs, and how to classify fix-ups as improvements or repairs. You will gain a thorough understanding of the new mortgage interest rules so you can maximize your interest deductions. You will also learn about one of the most overlooked deductions in the country: points. We discuss tax planning tips that you should know before building your own home, and finally, we reveal how to maximize your deductions for real estate taxes and avoid some of the traps.

3

Tax Basis–The Starting Place for All Deductions

The beginning is the most important part of the work.

—Plato

Your tax basis begins when you acquire real estate, and basis is the foundation for all future tax planning, whether for home ownership or for investment property. Basis is important for many tax purposes, such as determining gain or loss on disposition of all real estate, and basis is important in determining the amount of depreciation deductions for rental property.

Overview

1. Understand the importance of basis
2. Learn the factors that comprise basis
3. Learn how basis is affected by gifts and inheritance
4. Learn about the potential elimination of estate tax and how that can be a bombshell in computing basis

Sandy's elaboration: It is imperative that you document all items that increase your basis and keep careful records for proof of these expenditures. We discuss most of the factors that increase basis and exactly what you need to keep in Chapter 4.

The amount of your initial basis depends on how you acquire the property. Different rules apply to purchases, gifts, inheritances, and other special tax-oriented acquisitions such as like-kind exchanges. If this isn't complicated enough, your basis also changes while you own the property. For example, it is increased by acquisition costs and capital improvements. If it is rental property or a home where you have a home office, it is decreased by depreciation. The original basis after the adjustments during ownership has a simple name: adjusted basis. This concept is discussed in more detail in Chapter 5.

Example: Jim buys a home for $300,000. He makes no improvements during the time of his ownership. If he sells that home a year later for $400,000, he pays tax on $100,000 of gain—the difference between his selling price and his basis.

Example: If Jim bought a rental property for the same $400,000, his depreciation would be based on his basis.

Purchased Property

The basis of purchased property is its cost.[1] This includes not only the cash paid, but any amount of the purchase price financed by someone else. It doesn't matter whether the financing is from an outside institutional source or from a note carried by the seller.

Example: Vivian buys a home for $600,000. She gives $100,000 cash to the seller and gets a bank loan for $500,000. Her total basis is $600,000, which includes the loan and the cash. If the seller provided the loan instead of the bank, her basis would still be $600,000.

Sandy's elaboration: Inclusion of debt in basis gives real estate one of its greatest benefits. First, real estate has a greater potential for leverage than other investments. Second, using other people's money increases your basis for depreciation; thus you get valuable tax deductions without spending your own money!

Property Received as Gift

Generally, basis for the donee (person receiving the gift) is the same as basis for the donor (person making the gift), plus any gift tax paid by the donor.[2] This merely shifts the pregift gain from donor to donee.

Caution: Different rules apply if the fair market value of the property is less than the donor's basis at the time of the gift. If the fair market value of the property is less than the basis, you still use the donor's basis for figuring gain or for depreciation, but you use the fair market value for figuring loss. This is another fine example of tax simplification.

Example: As a gift, Karen receives a car that she uses in business. The car cost $28,000. Her basis for depreciation is $28,000. If the fair market value of the car at the time of the gift is $16,000, her basis in figuring gain or depreciation is still $28,000, but her basis for figuring loss is $16,000.

If Karen sells the car, she gets no loss deduction unless she sells it for less than the $16,000 fair market value. Her loss deduction is the difference between fair market value and sales price.

Property Received As Gift

Inherited Property

Generally, the basis of inherited property is its fair market value at the date of the decedent's death.[3] Notice that the decedent's original basis for the property is irrelevant.

Sandy's elaboration: This step-up in basis to market value means that the predeath appreciation in value is never subject to income tax. This opportunity to avoid tax highlights the importance of tax deferral. In other words, when you die, you win—at least for tax purposes! I admit that waiting for someone to die or having someone wait for me to die is not my favorite tax planning technique.

Example: Upon her mom's death, Sue inherits a home that is worth $800,000. Her mom and dad originally paid $100,000 for the property.

Sue's basis in the inherited property is $800,000, which is the fair market value.

Joint Property

Many times people inherit property that they owned jointly. The basis becomes one-half of what was paid for the property plus the fair market value of one-half interest.[4]

Example: Jack and his sister Jill own a home for which they paid $100,000. Each has a $50,000 original cost. If Jack dies when the property is worth $800,000, Jill's new basis in the property becomes $450,000—which is computed by taking her original $50,000 cost basis plus one-half of the fair market value upon Jack's death.

Sandy's elaboration: I should note that Congress plans to eliminate the Estate Tax in 2010. Should this happen, you'll have a major "gotcha." You will have to use the original basis of the property rather than the fair market value at death. Thus, you will need to know what the decedent's adjusted basis was before he died.

Your Castle and Your Tax Shelter

In addition to appreciation in value and the great opportunity for using leverage, home ownership offers tax benefits not available for any alternate form of investment. You must be aware of the tax implications at three points in your home ownership experience:

1. When you buy the home: Make sure that your records and tax strategies establish your initial tax basis so that later you can maximize your positive cash flow from tax savings alone.
2. While you own your home: Maximize the home mortgage interest and real estate tax deductions. You might also have other home-related deductions in special circumstances, such as casual losses.
3. When you dispose of your principal residence: Here is one of the greatest tax giveaways—the home sale exclusion. Be sure to know how the rules work to maximize your benefits. Also, you can structure a seller take-back note to substantially increase your wealth.

Summary

- Your basis is the starting point for calculating gains and losses and for figuring out depreciation. The basis will change over the years to account for improvements, which increase basis, and for depreciation, which decreases basis. This new basis is a result of future adjustments and is known as adjusted basis.

- Your original basis is generally your acquisition cost, which consists of any cash you paid and any liabilities you incurred.
- When you receive property by gift, your basis for gain, loss, and depreciation is generally the donor's adjusted basis.
- If the fair market value at the time of the gift is lower than the donor's original basis, your basis for gain and depreciation is still the donor's adjusted basis. Your basis for loss, however, is the fair market value as of the date of the gift.
- When you inherit property, your basis is the fair market value at the time of the decedent's death. By inheriting property, you avoid all predeath appreciation.
- If you inherit property that you owned jointly, your basis is what you paid for your original joint interest, plus the fair market value of the decedent's interest.
- In 2010, if Congress eliminates the estate tax, be careful of the basis, which becomes the original decedent's basis and not fair market value. This is a real whammy.

Notes

1 Section 1012 of the IRC
2 Section 1015 of the IRC
3 Section 1014 of the IRC
4 Section 1014 of the IRC and the Income Tax Regulations (Regs) thereunder

4

IRS Record-Keeping Requirements to Bulletproof Your Basis

The taxpayer—that's someone who works for the federal government but doesn't have to take a civil service examination.
—**Ronald Reagan**

The day you buy your first home is the day you must start keeping records to prove the tax basis in your home. Good records will help you pay the lowest tax upon sale of your home and will increase your basis for any possible depreciation. You need records of:

- Closing costs
- Improvements
- Appliances and fixtures
- Landscaping

Overview
1. Understand what records the IRS requires to bulletproof your basis for any property
2. Learn how long you need to keep these records
3. Understand the tax classification of each item found on the settlement sheet when you purchase a principal home or vacation home
4. Learn ways to get basis adjustments for some items that normally would not affect your basis

There is no substitute for good records. By keeping good purchase and home improvement records, you keep your tax to a minimum. You can do this without Herculean effort. Simply keep your home improvement receipts and invoices in a permanent file with your settlement papers.

Sandy's elaboration: I keep a file for each property I own that contains all receipts for improvements and a separate file for rental property repair receipts. In each file, I have a sheet that lists the expense, what it was for, the check number used (or credit card), and the date of the fix-up or improvement. I keep a running total of all my improvements because improvements are added to basis.

The sheet I keep in my improvement file looks like this:

Item	Amount	Date	Check#/CreditCard	Vendor
Two new toilets	$1,200	9/15/05	credit card	DRF Contractors

Sandy's tip: It is a good idea to update a carry-forward schedule of your basis each year. This update helps you remember what happened and generally helps maintain better records.

How Long to Keep Receipts

According to the IRS[1], you need to keep records on your home as long as they are important in figuring your basis. Isn't that helpful?!

When you sell your old home tax-free because your profit falls below the $250,000 exclusion limit ($500,000 for married filing jointly), you need the purchase and sales records on both the old home and the new home as well.[2]

Sandy's elaboration: What this generally means is that you need to keep your records of expenses for rental property at least six years after the year that you incur the expense. If the records are for improvements, basis adjustments, casualty losses, or depreciation, you need to keep those records that affect basis for as long as the property is owned by you and for six years after a taxable sale. Tax return information should be kept until the seas run dry. In other words, tax returns should be kept forever!

What Records Do You Specifically Need to Keep?

You should keep all records that relate to the basis of your home, which is why I have recommended a separate file and carry-forward schedule for all improvements made. The records you need include:

- Purchase contracts
- Settlement statements
- Receipts for improvements
- Canceled checks
- Prior tax returns
- Deductible expenses for property taxes and mortgage interest

Settlement and Closing Costs

Have you ever purchased a home and, at the closing table, you got a complicated sheet of settlement costs? Did you wonder how each of those things might affect your taxes or basis? Well, wonder no more. There are four ways to treat items on the settlement sheet. They can be added to your basis, they can be deductible, they can be amortized or written off over the life of the loan, or they can be completely nondeductible. Ugh! If they are deemed nondeductible, you don't get to add them to your basis and you get no deduction—you get no benefit whatsoever from these expenses.[3]

See Figure 4-1 for typical settlement costs and their tax treatment.

Tax Classification of Buyer's Settlement Statement Expenses

	TYPE OF PROPERTY	
	Investment	Principal home
Costs of obtaining title		
Real estate broker's commission	Basis	Basis
Finder's fees	Basis	Basis
Legal fees	Basis	Basis
Title search	Basis	Basis
Title policy charges	Basis	Basis
Title recording fees	Basis	Basis
Transfer (stamp) taxes	Basis	Basis
Survey	Basis	Basis
Costs incident to purchase		
Real estate taxes	Basis/Deduct	Basis/Deduct
Hazard insurance	Deduct	Nondeductible
Condominium fees	Deduct	Nondeductible
Utilities	Deduct	Nondeductible
Costs incident to loan		
Legal fees	Amortize	Nondeductible
Appraisal fees	Amortize	Nondeductible
Mortgage broker's commission	Amortize	Nondeductible
Pest inspection	Amortize	Nondeductible
Credit reports	Amortize	Nondeductible
Commitment fees	Amortize	Nondeductible
Loan fees (not points)	Amortize	Nondeductible
Mortgage insurance premiums	Deduct	Nondeductible
Costs representing prepayments of interest		
Points	Amortize	Deduct
Prepaid interest	Amortize	Deduct
VA and FHA points	Amortize	Deduct

Figure 4-1

Example: Carey buys a new home and incurs $4,000 of real estate commission to find the home, $500 legal fees, and $1,000 for the title policy. How much gets added to his basis? If you check the "Costs of obtaining title," you will see that the entire amount gets added to basis.

Example: Carey has to pay some prorated utilities and condominium fees of $300. How are these treated? These are found in "Costs incident to purchase" and are nondeductible.

Example: In order to get the bank loan, Carey has to pay $500 to the bank's attorneys, $400 for an appraisal, and $250 for pest inspection. How are these items treated? They are found in Figure 4-1, "Costs incident to loan," and are nondeductible.

Sandy's tip: If the seller pays a buyer's expense that is deductible, the buyer may claim the deduction and reduce the basis by that amount.

Example: Joan buys a home, paying $120,000 for it. If the seller paid $400 of Joan's property tax bill at closing, Joan may reduce her basis by $400 to $119,600 and deduct $400 as property taxes paid at closing even though these taxes were paid by the seller.

What Do We Do with Nondeductible Items?

As you can see from Figure 4-1, you can't deduct some settlement costs or add them to basis.[4] However, as I have said before, "where there is a will ... there is a lawyer."

Sandy's tip: Have the seller pay the loan costs and other nondeductible expenses that do not benefit the buyer (which would be offset by a slightly higher sales price). The seller treats the costs as selling expenses, thereby reducing gain from the sale. The buyer has no nondeductible cash outlays, but will get a higher basis because he or she is paying a bit more for the property. The bottom line effect is that this technique effectively allows these otherwise nondeductible items as basis additions.

Sandy's elaboration: If you aren't familiar with what the nondeductible loan costs could be, check with a lender to get an estimate before you sign a contract. This way you will know how much to raise the contract price to offset this amount. Points, as you will learn in Chapter 7, are deductible. Therefore you don't need the seller to pay points.

Example: Morgan agrees to sell her home to Lori for $300,000. Morgan's basis in the home is $100,000. The closing costs include legal fees of $500, a $400 survey, a $300 pest inspection, and title insurance of $800 (total of $2,000 in costs incident to the loan). If Lori pays these expenses, which is the case in most transactions, they are nondeductible to Lori, and Morgan's gain is $200,000 ($300,000 selling price less $100,000 basis). If Morgan pays these costs and Lori buys the house for $302,000, Morgan's gain gets reduced by $2,000 of loan costs, and the amount of gain is the same. Lori gets a step up in basis because she is paying Morgan $2,000 more for the house. Everyone wins except the IRS.

Caution: Make sure the purchase price isn't so far out of line with the appraisal that you jeopardize bank financing.

Summary

- Having a high basis will reduce future gain on sales and increase any potential depreciation.
- You need to keep certain records forever. For improvements, you should keep a carry-forward schedule and file for all improvements and receipts.
- Keep all receipts for closing costs, improvements, appliances, landscaping, property taxes, and interest. If you own rental property, keep these plus all repair expenses and insurance costs.

- Check Figure 4-1 as to how to treat each item in your settlement statement. Remember, loan closing costs on homes are generally nondeductible (other than for points) and are not added to basis.
- Have the seller pay the nondeductible items, since it is a wash to the seller, and raise the contract price to account for these items. Sometimes you don't know exactly how much these may be, so get an estimate from the lender.

Notes

1 IRS Publication 530, *Tax Information for First time Homeowners* and IRS Publication 552, *Recordkeeping for Individuals*
2 Sections 1011, 1012, 121, 6001, 6501 of the IRC
3 Section 1016 of the IRC, see also IRS publications 530, and 522, noted above
4 IRS Publication 17, *Your Federal Income Tax-Individuals*, and IRS Publication 530, *Tax Information for First Time Homeowners*

5

Why Making Improvements to Your Home Is Much More Valuable than Making Repairs

I'm proud to be paying taxes in the United States. The only thing is—I could be just as proud for half the money.
—Arthur Godfrey

As you have learned, having a high adjusted basis is very beneficial because you are only taxed on the sales price that exceeds your adjusted basis. Also, the adjusted basis is used for any depreciation calculations. Improvements are one of those adjustments that increase your adjusted basis.

During the time that you own and occupy your home, you will spend money to repair and improve it. You also get itemized deductions for home mortgage interest and real estate taxes. All these cash expenditures have twists and turns that you must understand to maximize your tax benefits. These twists and turns aren't necessarily complicated, but you do need to understand what to do. Additionally, if your home is damaged by fire, storm, etc., you may have a casualty loss deduction.

Overview

1. Understand that home improvements add to your basis, in contrast to repairs, which don't affect basis
2. Learn some criteria that the IRS uses to classify fix-up expenditures as improvements
3. Learn why making fix-ups part of a general plan of improvements can be very beneficial
4. Understand why you should keep receipts for most appliances
5. Understand how landscaping affects improvements and learn about the 20-foot rule as it applies to landscaping
6. Understand the formula for computing adjusted basis for real property

31

Strategy: Make improvements that add to basis. With regard to taxes, you don't want to fix up your home; you want to improve it. Repairs are considered personal expenses, are not deductible, and are not added to basis. They are useless when incurred in your principal residence or second home. An improvement, however, adds value to your home—not to mention increases your tax basis.

Tests for Improvements

When you fix up your home, how do you know when that expenditure is a repair or an improvement? A review of tax cases has noted a number of similar factors that both the courts and the IRS look for when determining whether a fix-up is an improvement:

1. An improvement adds value to your home.
2. Improvements considerably prolong its useful life.
3. Improvements adapt an item to some new use.
4. Improvements fix whole walls or roofs, whereas repairs fix parts of walls and roofs.

Sandy's elaboration: The main key to whether something is a repair or an improvement is determined by whether it is new or not. New doors would be an improvement, but repairing the door or door handle would be a repair. The following have been held by the courts to be improvements:

- New doors[1]
- New iron grills on windows[2]
- New skylights[3]
- New windows[4]
- New permanent partitions[5]
- New roofs[6] (although some courts have held this to be repairs)[7]
- New floors[8]
- Rewiring[9]

You may have hundreds of improvements. Some may seem minor, but when taken together, they can add much to your basis. Improvements that may seem minor at the time include:

- Building new shelves in the pantry
- Constructing a bird bath on the patio
- Refinishing your kitchen with new cabinet doors
- Adding phone, cable jacks, or other outlets

Capitalize Water & Fertilizer

Hot tip: Make fix-ups part of a general plan of improvement, and you will add to your home basis.[10] If you combine what would be a repair as part of a general plan of improvements, both the IRS and the tax court have agreed that this whole expenditure becomes an improvement.

Example: Jeff wants to fix and clean some gutters on his roof, which would ordinarily be considered a repair. However, if he makes these repairs part of a new roof contract, the whole project is considered an improvement.

Sandy's elaboration: The strategy for improvement to rental property is exactly the opposite from that of your home. For rental property (whether it is residential rental or commercial property), repairs may be deducted in the year they are made. Unlike with homes, repairs are not ignored as personal expenses when incurred on investment property. Therefore, the strategy for investment properties is to work in such a way that they are not improvements, but deductible repairs. This aspect of rental property ownership is fully discussed in Chapter 22.

Special Assessments

Special assessments are those assessments made by state and local governments for improvements to streets, sidewalks, etc. They are added to your basis and are not deductible as a tax.[11]

Appliances and Fixtures

You also get to add to your basis built-in appliances or fixtures and appliances that transfer with the house, even if not built into the house, such as:[12]

- Bookcases
- Sinks
- Lighting fixtures
- Refrigerators
- Stoves
- Dishwashers
- Fire and burglar alarms
- Cabinets and storage sheds
- Television antenna and wiring
- Washers and dryers
- Automatic garage doors

Landscaping: Improvements include the cost of establishing a lawn, hedge, or planting a tree. Common examples of landscaping improvements include:

- Terraces
- Gardens
- Play areas
- Fences (including surveys)[13]
- Retaining walls
- Sprinkler systems
- Barbecue pits
- Swimming pools
- Topsoil walkways
- Lamp posts
- Driveways
- Fill
- Tennis courts
- Seed, bulbs, and vines

Sandy's tip: Don't forget to capitalize the cost of water and fertilizer used to establish new grass and plants.[14]

Twenty-feet rule: All landscaping gets added to the basis of the building when it's generally within 20 feet of the building. If the landscaping is more than 20 feet from the building, the costs get added to the basis of the land. This is important later on if you depreciate the property.

Overall Basis Formula

As you have learned, you get to increase your original basis by improvements you make. However, there are some items that decrease your basis, such as:

- Any gain on sales of prior homes when you deferred tax (such as being a result of a like-kind exchange).[15]
- Depreciation claimed while the home was rented or when you claimed a home office.[16]
- Payments received by you for granting an easement or right of way for a company to use your property. This is generally granted to utilities.[17]
- The net tax deduction that you claimed for a casualty loss after any reimbursement for insurance.[18]

The formula for figuring your adjusted basis is as follows:

Adjusted basis = cost + improvements – any deferred gain from sale of old home – depreciation allowed or allowable – payments received for right of way – net tax deduction for casualty loss

Summary

- It is usually very beneficial to have your adjusted basis as high as possible in order to minimize gains, maximize losses, and maximize depreciation.
- For principal residences and second homes, try to classify fix-up expenses as improvements.
- For rental properties, you are better off classifying fix-up expenses as repairs because they are deductible when incurred in investment properties.
- Improvements add value to the property. You have improvements when you extend the property's useful life, use better materials, or fix whole parts of a wall or item instead of part of a wall or item.
- Generally, new items are improvements. Fixing part of an item is a repair.
- Combine fix-ups as part of a general plan of improvements in order to make the whole project qualify as an improvement.
- Special assessments are deemed improvements and, as such, are added to basis.
- Landscaping generally constitutes improvements to the land. However, if a hedge or tree is added within 20 feet of the building, it would constitute a building improvement.
- Improvements increase basis. Depreciation, casualty losses, and payments for easements reduce basis.

Notes

1 *Alabama-Georgia Syrup Company vs. Comm.*, 36 TC 747(1961), Rev'd on another issue, 63-1 USTC 9124 (5th Cir. 1963)

2 *The Fidelity Storage Corporation vs.Burnet*, 58 F.2d 526 (DC Cir. 1932)

3 *St.Louis Malleable Casting Company vs. Comm.*, 9 BTA 110 (1927)

4 *Ben T. Wright, Inc., vs. Comm.*, 12 BTA 1149(1928)

5 *Farenga vs. Comm.*, 14 TCM 1087 (1955)

6 *Ibid*

7 *Thurner vs. Commissioner*, 11 T.C.M. 42 (1952, and *Oberman Mfg. Co. vs. Comm,* 47 T.C. 471 (1967), acq., 1967-2 C.B. 3

8 *Mountain State Steel Foundries, Inc. vs. Comm.*, 18 TCM 306 (1959), Rev'd on other issues, 60-2 USTC 9797 (4th Cir. 1960)

9 *Lycoming Silk Company vs. Comm.*, 11 BTA 523 (1928)

10 *Bane v. Comm.*, TC Memo 1971-31, *Seahill Company v. Comm.*, 23 TCM 408 (1964). See also IRS Publication 530, *Tax Information for First Time Homeowners*

11 Sections 164 © (1) and 1016(a) of the IRC. See also Sections 1.164-2 and 1-164-4 of the ITR

12 IRS Publication 17, *Your Federal Income Tax-for Individuals (2004)*

13 IRS Publication 530, *Tax Information for First Time Homeowners*

14 *Algernon Blair, Inc.*, 29 TC 1205 (1957)

15 Sections 1016(a)(7) of the IRC and section 1.1016-5(d) of the Regs

16 Sections 167(a)(1), 1011, 1016 (a)(2) of the IRC

17 Section 1016 of the IRC, section 1.1016-2 of the Regs, Rev. Rul. 68-291, 1968-1 CB 351 and Rev. Rul. 73-161, 1973-1 CB 366

18 Section 1016(a)

6

Maximizing the New Mortgage Interest Rules

Blessed are the young, for they shall inherit the national debt.

—Herbert Hoover

Most people believe you can deduct any interest, especially interest incurred on your home. This myth is only partially true. There are now six types of interest. They are:

- Business interest (usually deductible in full)
- Investment interest (deductible against investment income)
- Passive interest (deals with rental property)
- Personal interest (usually nondeductible)
- Construction interest (interest incurred in connection with your home being built)
- Home mortgage interest (includes two types of interest—acquisition debt interest and home equity debt interest)

Overview
1. Understand that there are six different categories of interest
2. Understand what interest you can deduct for your qualified home
3. Learn the basics of vacation home rules
4. Learn about home equity and hybrid debt
5. Understand how financed improvements may increase your acquisition debt interest for deductibility
6. Learn how the AMT affects your mortgage interest deduction
7. Learn about the tax consequences of renting out a room in your home

Sandy's elaboration: Each of these types of interest is treated separately and has different rules. It is hard to believe that Congress was so stupid as to allow this situation!

37

General Rule

You may deduct interest paid on the acquisition and home equity debt secured by both a qualified principal home or second home.[1] You must also be the person who is liable on the debt. Thus, you can't deduct interest that you pay on your kid's mortgage unless you were also jointly liable on the debt.

To deduct interest on acquisition or home equity debt, you must make the payments, and your qualified home must secure the debt.[2]

Example: Tina takes out a loan on some investments to pay for the down payment on her new principal residence. None of the interest on this loan qualifies as home mortgage interest because the loan was not secured by her principal residence.

What Is a Qualified Home?

In order to deduct home mortgage interest, you must have a loan that is secured by a qualified home. A qualified home means:[3]

- Your principal home, which is the home that you live in for most of the year
- One second home selected by you for purposes of deducting home mortgage interest.[4]

Sandy's elaboration: Notice that you can deduct certain home mortgage interest incurred on your primary home and on one second home of your choosing. You cannot deduct home mortgage interest on more than one second home. You can choose which second home is to be treated as a qualified home, which leads us to the following strategy:

Sandy's tip: If you own several second or vacation homes, pick the second home that gives you the best interest deduction.[5]

Example: Donald owns several vacation homes. For one home he pays $8,000 a year in interest. For his vacation home, he pays $6,000 interest in a year. Donald would elect the first as the qualified second home because he gets a bigger interest deduction. This election can be made each year.

Sometimes people rent out their second or vacation home, which can raise the question as to whether it is a qualified second home or is a rental property. Congress actually thought of this and came out with a formula for you to determine which is which.

You may treat your second home as a qualified home for the year, even if you rent it out for part of the year, if you use it for personal purposes for more than the greater of:[6]

- 14 days
- 10 percent of the days that you rent it out

Sandy's elaboration: What this formula means is that you can rent out your vacation home and still treat it as a second residence for home mortgage deductions if you don't rent it out for too long a period of time.

Example: Barbara owns a vacation home that she rents out during part of the season for 21 days. She uses the vacation home for 60 days when she and her family live there. Let's see what happens. To meet the test, she must use the home personally for the greater of 14 days or 10 percent of the days rented out. Because her personal use is 60 days, she meets the test for qualifying as a second home.

Part of the Democratic tax reform package is to eliminate the deduction for second home interest. Be aware of this potential problem.

What Is a Home?

Your principal residence or second home can be a house, apartment, condominium, motor home, mobile home, house trailer, boat, or other property that provides basic living accommodations such as a sleeping place, a toilet, and

cooking facilities.[7] Your home may even be stock in a cooperative housing corporation held by you as a tenant-shareholder.[8]

Acquisition Debt

Because you now know that you can deduct interest in acquisition debt for your qualified home, the next question is what is acquisition debt? I'm glad you asked. Acquisition debit is both:

- Incurred to purchase, construct, or substantially improve any qualified home
- Secured by that home[9]

In addition, and this is the kicker, you must reduce your acquisition debt as you make principal payments. You can only increase your acquisition debt on a property when you use the proceeds to make substantial improvements to the home.[10]

Example: Jane buys a home for $800,000, taking out a first mortgage for $700,000, which is secured by the home as collateral. This debt clearly qualifies as acquisition debt. If Jane pays down the mortgage and refinances the debt, the new refinanced debt still qualifies as acquisition debt.

What Congress giveth, Congress taketh away. There is an overall maximum limit on acquisition debt incurred after October 13 ($1,000,000 for married filing jointly or $500,000 married filing separately).[11]

Home Equity Debt

In addition to the interest on acquisition debit for both your home and a second home, you can deduct interest on home equity debt secured by a qualified home. Generally, the maximum amount of home equity debt is $100,000, but if the net equity of your home is less, you can only deduct interest up to your net equity. Your net equity is the fair market value of your home less all mortgages outstanding.

Sandy's elaboration: Because you can deduct the interest on up to one million dollars of acquisition debt in addition to $100,000 of home equity debt, the total amount of debt that you can deduct interest on a home would be $1.1 million. Thus, if you buy a home for $2,000,000, using bank financing of $1,600,000, you can deduct the interest on $1.1 million of the $1.6 million of debt. The remaining interest would be personal interest and would be nondeductible. Ugh!

Example: Martin owns a home worth $500,000 but has mortgages on the home that total $450,000. His net equity is $50,000, which is the difference between the fair market value of the home and the total mortgages on the home. If he were to take a home equity loan on the home of $100,000, his ability to deduct the interest on home equity debt would be $50,000 because that is his net equity. If his net equity were $100,000 or more, he could deduct the interest on the full $100,000.

Compliance tip: If you buy a home where the seller provides financing, you must provide on your tax return the seller's name, address, and Social Security number.

Hybrid Debt

Sometimes a single mortgage may be a hybrid debt—part acquisition debt, part home-equity debt, and part other debt.[12] Usually the interest on the other debt is nondeductible unless you can show that the money was used for investment or business purposes. The following example illustrates this.

Example: Michelangelo buys a home, incurring a $900,000 mortgage. When his mortgage balance is $500,000, he refinances and takes out a $800,000 mortgage. His original acquisition debt is still $500,000, and his home equity debt is $100,000. Thus, $600,000 of this refinanced debt would be considered home mortgage debt, while the remaining $200,000 would be considered personal debt. However, if he uses $150,000 of the refinancing to build an improvement, he can add this $150,000 to his acquisition debt and deduct the interest on this portion as well. The remaining $50,000 would be considered personal debt, which leads to nondeductible interest.

Sandy's elaboration: If Michelangelo used the remaining $50,000 to fund his business ventures, he could deduct the interest on this remaining business debt as well.

Sandy's tip: When you refinance your home for more than the acquisition debt and home equity limit of $100,000, you must show where you used the money. If it was used for an improvement in your home or for business, the interest would be deductible. Therefore, keep documents that prove you borrowed the money to make improvements or used the money for your business. Keep the money in a separate checking, savings, or money market account so that you have an audit trail.

Alternative Minimum Tax: Here is one of the "gotchas" Congress foisted on us in the AMT. You can't deduct home equity mortgage interest for the AMT, which means if you finance your second home with a home equity loan on your principal residence, you can't deduct the interest on that home equity loan. This is not only true for a house or an apartment that you use as a second home but also for qualifying second home yachts, motor homes, and house trailers.[13]

Bedroom Rentals

For purposes of interest deduction, if you rent out part of your principal or second home, you may treat the rental portion as your qualifying home if:[14]

- The tenant uses the rented portion as a home
- The rented portion lacks separate cooking or toilet facilities
- You rent to less than two tenants (persons sharing sleeping quarters, such as a husband and wife, count as one tenant).

The advantage of treating the bedroom rental as part of your qualifying home is that you get to deduct the interest in full as qualifying home mortgage interest. You reduce your rental expenses for interest claimed as home mortgage interest. With the reduction, you may be able to escape the passive loss restrictions.

Summary

- There are six different types of interest that are treated separately, each having different rules for deductibility.
- You may deduct interest paid on the acquisition debt of your home and one second home (up to 1 million dollars) and up to $100,000 of home equity debt.
- If you have more than one vacation or second home, pick the one each year that gives you the most deductions.
- A qualified home can be a house, house boat, condominium, or co-op. Your principal home is where you live the majority of the year.
- If you rent out your second home, you may still qualify the acquisition debt or home equity debt as home mortgage debt if your personal use exceeds the greater of 14 days or 10 percent of days rented.
- If you refinance your home, you may have hybrid debt, which could be a combination of several types of interest, some of which may be deductible. It is essential to document the use of the proceeds with canceled checks and to keep the money in a separate account so that you have an audit trail.
- Watch out for the Alternative Minimum Tax (AMT). If you are subject to AMT, you may not deduct any interest on home-equity debt, but you can deduct interest on acquisition debt.
- If you rent out a room in your home, you might be able to treat the whole house as a qualifying home if you meet certain tests. This would allow full

deductibility of interest and prevent the passive loss rules from applying to your rented portion.

Notes

1 Section 163 (h)(3) of the IRC
2 Section 1.163-10T (j)(1) of the Temp Regs
3 Section 163 (h)(4)(i) of the IRC
4 Section 163 (h)(4)(A) of the IRC
5 Section 163 (h)(4)(A)(i) of the IRC
6 Section 163 (h)(4)(A) of the IRC
7 Section 1.163-10T (p)(3)(ii) of the Temp Regs
8 Section 163 (h)(4)(B) of the IRC
9 Section 163 (h)(3)(b) of the IRC
10 HR. Rep. No. 391 (PT.II), 100th Cong. 1st Session 1033 (1987)
11 Section 163 (h)(3)(B)(i) of the IRC
12 IRS Notice 88-74, 1988-2 CB 383
13 Section 56 (b)(1)(C) of the IRC
14 Section 1.163-10T(p)(4)(ii) of the Temp Regs and IRS Publication 936, *Home Mortgage Interest Deduction (2004)*

7

The Point of Points

The meek shall inherit the earth.
–The Bible

But they shall also overpay their taxes.
–Sandy Botkin

Overview
1. Understand the importance of points
2. Learn the difference in treatment of points when incurred on your principal home versus that of a second home or investment property
3. Understand the effect of seller-paid points

In my prior book, *Lower Your Taxes— BIG TIME* (published by McGraw-Hill), I noted that one of the top four overlooked real estate deductions dealt with points. It is truly amazing how often I find people not taking their rightful deductions in this area. This chapter literally can put thousands in your pocket based on overlooked deductions.

What are points? Points are what you pay to get a loan. They are normally classified as prepaid interest. To be eligible as points, they must be classified as either points, prepaid interest, or loan origination fees on your settlement statement. A point is 1 percent of your loan. Thus, if you pay two points in order to obtain a $100,000 loan, you pay $2,000.

Home Buyer Points

You may deduct the points you pay to either purchase or improve your principal home in the year that you pay them provided:[1]

1. Your down payment exceeds the charge for the points.
2. Your principal home secures your loan.

45

3. Charging points is an established practice in the geographic area where the loan is made.
4. Points charged do not exceed the usual charge for points in that area.

 Sandy's elaboration: From the above tests, you should note that you can only deduct points paid on loans that are secured by your principal residence and that points are not immediately deductible when incurred on rental property or second homes. In addition, the points need to be paid for loans that are used to either purchase your home or to make improvements to your home. If you refinance a loan to get a better rate, these points are not immediately deductible. Such points must be deducted ratably over the life of the loan.

Points Need Not Be Paid in Cash

Under an IRS ruling, you may deduct points even if you did not pay the points in cash, such as when points are withheld from the loan proceeds.[2] However, you can only claim the deduction if the money that you bring to the settlement (down payment, recording taxes, etc.) exceeds the charge for the points.

Example: Sandra has to pay $4,000 in points. She finances most of the loan, and she puts down a $2,500 deposit. Sandra may deduct only $2,500 of the points.

I should note that the IRS has changed its position over the years regarding VA and FHA origination fees. It now says that you may deduct as points any VA or FHA origination fees paid after December 31, 1990.[3]

Seller-Paid Points

What happens if the seller pays some or all of the points? Points paid by the seller are treated as a selling expense by the seller and thus reduce the amount realized from the sale of the home.[4] Any points paid by the seller for the purchase of a principal residence of the buyer may also be deducted by the buyer if the buyer reduces the basis for the home by the amount of the points paid by the seller.[5]

Example: For $200,000 Joan sells to Marc a home that will be his principal residence. Joan pays two points of $4,000. Joan's amount realized from the sale is $196,000 ($200,000 less the $4,000 in points paid). Marc may deduct the points but must reduce his adjusted basis for the house to $196,000 ($200,000 cost less $4,000 in seller-paid points).

Other Points

We discussed points incurred on your principal residence for the purchase or improvement of that residence. What about all other points, such as:

- Points paid for refinancing any property that does not involve either the purchase or improvement of a home
- Points paid for second homes or vacation homes
- Points paid for investment property such as for residential rental property

The Rule

If you pay points to obtain a loan for any of the above-noted reasons, you amortize the points over the life of the loan. This means that you write off the points in equal amounts over the life of the loan.[6] This is also the treatment of points that you pay to refinance any mortgage, including a mortgage to refinance your principal residence.

Example: Martha pays $3,600 in points when she refinances her home to get a lower interest rate on a 30-year loan. She writes off the points at the rate of $10 per month over the 360 months of the mortgage.

Tax Planning Strategy

When you pay off a mortgage, deduct any unamortized points. Most people who incur points that are not immediately deductible forget to amortize the points over the life of the loan. Even worse, most people generally keep a loan for seven years or less. They either sell the home or refinance the loan.

What happens to the unamortized portion of the loan? The answer is that when you either refinance the loan or sell the home, you get to deduct all of the unamortized points. Most people miss this because they incurred the points many years ago and have forgotten about them. It is thus crucial to look at your settlement statements to see if you incurred any nondeductible points for the current loans on your property.

Example: Interest rates drop again. Martha refinances the old loan with a new lender. Two-and-a-half years ago, she paid $3,600 in points on a 30-year mortgage. With the payoff of the old mortgage, she writes off the $3,300 remainder (which is $10 multiplied by 330 remaining months). However, Martha must prorate any points incurred for the new refinanced loan over the life of the new loan.

Summary

- Points are charges paid to obtain a loan. They are generally considered points when the settlement statement classifies them as points, origination fees, or prepaid interest.
- One point means 1 percent of the mortgage amount.
- A home buyer can immediately deduct points if they are used to purchase or improve his or her principal residence.
- Points need not be paid in cash. They can be financed. However, your deduction for points is limited to the lesser of the amount of the points or the cash provided by the buyer at the settlement table. This includes any cash down payment or cash for property taxes and fees.
- Any seller-paid points are deducible by both the buyer and the seller. What a great country!
- Points incurred for refinancing any mortgage, to purchase a second home, or to purchase investment property must be amortized over the life of the loan.
- Don't forget to deduct all unamortized points when you either refinance the old loan or you sell the property that the old loan was based on.

Notes

1 Section 461 (g)(2) of the IRC
2 Rev. Proc. 92-12, 1992-1 CB 663
3 Rev. Proc. 92-12A, 1992-1 CB 664
4 Rev. Rul. 68-650, 1968-2 CB 78
5 Rev. Proc. 94-27, 1994 CB 613
6 Section 461 (g)(1) of the IRC

8

Maximizing Your Deductions when Building a Home

People who complain about taxes can be divided into two classes: men and women.

–Anonymous

As you remember from Chapter 6, there are six types of interest. Personal interest is not deductible.[1] Interest on your home mortgage is deductible.[2] Therefore, it makes sense that when you build your home you want:

- Home mortgage interest
- No personal interest

> **Overview**
> 1. Learn about the construction period interest rules when building a home
> 2. Understand why you should have a performance bond when you contract to have a home built
> 3. Understand the documentation you need to prove that your intent was to build a home rather than investment property

If you are going to build a home on raw land to your specifications, this will be a very useful chapter.

This chapter will be especially beneficial for real estate or investment professionals who specialize in tract or raw land sales.

Big Break–Construction Period Interest

Tax law gives you a break. If you buy raw land with the intent to build your home, you may treat up to 24 months of construction period interest as deductible home mortgage interest if the home that you build becomes a qualified home on the first day that it is ready for occupancy.[3]

Sandy's tip: To ensure that your interest is deductible, plan to buy the raw land and build your home within 24 months of the original financing of the land. Obtain a mortgage that covers the land and improvements, including property that you build. Spend a few minutes with a mortgage banker discussing the transaction before you or your clients buy the land.

Sandy's elaboration: It is to your benefit to have a penalty clause in the builder's contract that your home must be finished within a set time frame. If the home is not finished within the 24-month period of your purchase of the land, at least you will get some penalties to pay for your lost interest deductions.

Sandy's tip: If construction will take more than 24 months from the date of purchase of the land, select what you think will be the 24 months that will give you the greatest interest deduction. The 24 months can start any time on or after the day construction begins.[4]

Example: Your construction loan varies with prime rate. You get the best deduction when you pick the 24-month period with the highest charges for interest.

Interest on Land

If you buy raw land and pay interest on it in order to build rental property, the interest is investment interest that is only deductible to the extent of investment income.[5] If you change your mind and decide to build a home on the land, clearly document the change to make sure you can deduct both your investment and home mortgage interest.

Sandy's elaboration: If you incur investment interest, there is no time limit on your carryover of disallowed investment interest deductions.[6]

Documentation strategy: When you convert land from investment use to personal home use, you need proof. You can prove this desire to build a home on the land with the architect's drawing. The date of the contract with the architect helps prove the date you converted the land from investment to personal use.

Sandy's elaboration: Developers treat preconstruction period interest as interest arising from a trade or business.

Sandy's tip: If you are building a home to your specifications and not simply buying into a development, consider obtaining a performance bond. This is a bond provided by a financial institution that guarantees that the house will be completed if the developer fails to finish the job. If the developer has a strike, goes bankrupt, or has unforeseen circumstances, the financial institution guarantees that the house will be completed. The cost of a performance bond is approximately 2 percent of the purchase price of the home.

Summary

- When you build a house on raw land, you can deduct preconstruction-period interest by using any 24-month period of interest and home mortgage interest. Moreover, you can elect the period that produces the most interest.
- Try to have your house built within 24 months of the purchase of the land.
- If you incur interest on the purchase of the raw land for investment, you can deduct investment interest against investment income. Any excess can be carried over forever against future investment income.
- If you originally buy land in order to build rental property but change your plans to building a home, document this change with the architect's drawings and a contract.
- Consider a performance bond when you are building a home. This is especially true if your home is not part of a development.

Notes

1 Section 163 (h)(1) of the IRC
2 Section 163 (h)(3) of the IRC and see Chapter 6 of this book.
3 Section 1.163-10T (p)(5) of the Temp Regs
4 IRS Publications 936, *Home Mortgage Interest Deduction (2004)*
5 Section 163 (d) of the IRC
6 Section 163 (d)(2) of the IRC

9

Maximizing the Effect of Real Estate Taxes

Abracadabra, thus we learn
The more you create, the less you earn.
The less you earn, the more you're given,
The less you lead, the more you're driven,
The more destroyed, the more they feed,
The more you pay, the more they need,
The more you earn, the less you keep,
And now I lay me down to sleep.
I pray the Lord my soul to take
If the tax-collector hasn't got it before
I wake.

–Ogden Nash

Overview
1. Understand the general deduction rule regarding real estate taxes
2. Learn why you must allocate real property taxes based on ownership
3. Understand how the AMT can adversely affect you
4. Learn how to treat special assessments
5. Understand the tax treatment of transfer taxes and recording fees

You are allowed an itemized deduction for real estate taxes on your home and vacation homes.[1] Charges for improvements allocated to specific property owners who are benefited (special assessments) are not deductible as taxes, as discussed below.

Allocation in the Year of Sale

You may deduct only the amount of real estate taxes applicable to the number of days during the year that you own the property. This is true whether or not the taxes are prorated on the settlement sheet. Even though you pay the entire tax for the year and don't prorate, the amount of your

55

deduction is limited to the amount applicable to the part of the year that you own the property.[2]

Example: The real estate tax year is April 1 to March 31. Joan, the owner on April 1, 2006, sells the property to William on June 30, 2006. The property was sold 90 days into the real estate tax year. William owns the property throughout the rest of the tax year, which is from June 30 through March 31, 2007. The real estate tax for the tax year April 1, 2006 through March 31, 2007 is $3,650. Joan's deduction is limited to the amount deemed to be imposed on her: $900 (90/365 times $3,650). The remaining $2,750 is deemed to be imposed on William, and his deduction is limited to this amount.

Sandy's elaboration: Notice that your real estate deduction is prorated based on the days you own the property. This allocation is done on a daily basis.

What Happens If There Was No Prorating?

If you, as the buyer, pay more in taxes than what your prorated portion would be, the nondeductible tax is a capital expenditure that you add to your basis for determining your gain or loss.[3]

If you are the seller and pay more than your prorated share, you add the nondeductible portion to your basis, which will reduce your gain. If you paid and deducted the tax in a prior year, you must report the nondeductible part as ordinary income in the sale and add it to the basis of the property sold.[4]

Example: John purchases a home from Jim. Jim owns the property 90 days into the tax year. Thus, John owns the home 275 days of the tax year. By mistake, John pays the full $3,650 in taxes. Because he can only deduct $2,750, the extra nondeductible $900 gets added to his basis.

Sandy's tip: I can't think of any reason why you would want to pay more of the taxes than what is deductible. Most contracts with realtors take this into account. However, if you are not using a standard realtor's contract, you need to build in a clause that you, the buyer, will pay only the taxes based on prorating them for the year.

Special Assessments

When local governments install improvements, such as driveways and street improvements, and charge the benefited property owners their share of the cost, these charges are called special assessments. These are not deductible as real estate taxes. They get added to the basis of your property.[5]

Sandy's tip: Although not deductible, don't forget to add these to your basis.

Transfer and Recording Fees

Many states require transfer taxes and recording fees before a title can be recorded. If these are paid by the buyer, which is the usual case, they get added to the basis of the property. If they are paid by the seller, they are selling expenses that reduce the amount realized.[6]

Alternative Minimum Tax

Uncle Sam strikes again! You cannot deduct any state or local taxes, including real estate taxes for calculating AMT. If you live in a state with high state income and property taxes, the denial of this deduction could make you subject to the AMT. See your accountant about whether you may be subject to AMT. Generally, unless you have a lot of employee business expenses or qualified stock options or lots of long-term capital gains, you probably won't be subject to AMT.

Itemized Deduction Phaseout

Property taxes and interest on your home are deductible as itemized deductions.[7] However, in the year 2006, if you made over $150,500 of adjusted gross income and filed married filing jointly (this figure was reduced to $75,250 for married filing separately), you lost $200 of itemized deductions for every $10,000 you earned over these amounts. You should be aware of this problem.

Sandy's elaboration: This elimination of some itemized deductions, such as interest and taxes on your homes, does not apply to rental property expenses.

Summary

- You may claim as an itemized deduction all real property taxes on your principal and second home.
- Real property taxes are deductible based on the prorated days that you owned the property during the state's assessed tax year, which may not begin on January 1.
- If you pay more than what would be prorated to you based on the days of ownership of the property, any excess gets added to your basis.
- Special assessments are not considered real estate taxes but are benefits to specific owners that are levied by the local government. Special assessments must be added to your basis.
- Transfer taxes and recording fees get added to the basis of your home.
- If you are subject to alternative minimum tax (AMT), you can't deduct any real property taxes in computing what you owe for AMT. Check with your accountant to see if you are subject to AMT.
- Watch out for phaseout of itemized deductions if you earn too much money. In 2006 and 2007, you can have up to two-thirds of your itemized deductions eliminated by the phaseout.

Notes

1 Section 164 (a)(1) of the IRC
2 Section 164 (d)(1) of the IRS and section 1.164-6 (c) of the Regs
3 Section 1012 of the IRC and section 1.1012-1(b) of the Regs
4 Sections 1.164- 6(d)(5) and 1.1001-1(b)
5 Sections 164 ©(1), and (b)(2) of the IRC. See also section 1.164-4 of the Regs
6 Rev. Rul. 65-313, 1965-2 CB 47
7 See instructions for IRS Form 1040, Schedule A

Part 3

Maximizing Tax Benefits when You Dispose of Your Home

This part explains the Universal Exclusion requirements, which enable you avoid up to $500,000 of gain on the sale of your home every two years. We discuss some exceptions to the general rule, and we cover ways to get a huge step up in basis for your home and a depreciation deduction by having a very simple change in ownership. Yet you still keep control of your property.

10

Excluding Gain when You Sell Your Home–An Overview of the New Universal Exclusion

We have long had death and taxes as the two standards of inevitability. But there are those who believe that death is the preferable of the two. "At least," as one man said, "there's one advantage about death; it doesn't get worse every time Congress meets."

–Erwin N. Griswold

Overview
1. Understand the legal requirements for the Universal Exclusion, in which you will avoid up to $500,000 in gain
2. Learn the timing requirements of both ownership and residency in order to meet the exclusion
3. Learn why this exclusion is also called by accountants, "the home handy-man relief act" and "the itinerant landlord's relief act"
4. Learn why you might want to elect out of the exclusion

Y ou might have learned years ago that you could avoid gain from the sale of your home by purchasing another home of equal value. You also may have learned that if you were over age 55, you could have avoided up to $125,000 in gain. In order to simplify the law dealing with the sale of residences,[1] both of these rules were eliminated in 1997 and replaced with the Universal Exclusion.

The general rule is that you may exclude $250,000 of gain from the sale of your principal residence if you owned or used it as your principal residence for any two out of the last five years.[2] If you are married and

61

file jointly, you may exclude up to $500,000 of gain if you meet all of the following:

1. You or your spouse owned the residence for at least two of the last five years[3].
2. Both you and your spouse used the house as your principal residence for two of the last five years.[4]
3. Neither spouse is ineligible because he or she used the exclusion within the last two years[5].

 Sandy's elaboration: You should note that eligibility for the $500,000 exclusion not only requires that you or your spouse own the residence for two of the last five years, but also that both of you live in it for two of the last five years.

Example: Julie just married Patrick, who has owned and lived in his home for the past three years. If Julie moves in with Patrick, who sells the home one year later, they may only claim exclusion up to $250,000 because she didn't make Patrick's home her principal residence for at least two of the last five years.

Two-Out-of-Five-Year Requirement

This ownership and use test is strictly applied, with some exceptions to be discussed below. To use the automatic $250,000/$500,000 exclusion, either you or your spouse must have owned the residence and used it as your principal residence for any two of the last five years.[6] Your "ownership" period may differ from your "use" period as long as you satisfy both tests within the previous five-year window. Like the prior law, the two-year requirements need not be consecutive.[7] You can even count short absences for vacations as periods of use even if you rent out the home.[8]

Example: Colin rents and lives in a home in year one. In year two, he buys the home and lives in it until the end of the year. In year three, Colin moves out and rents the home to Sarah until the end of year five, when he sells it. Colin has:

- Owned the home for two of the past five years
- Used it as his principal residence for two of the past five years

The result is that he qualifies for the exclusion. Notice that the two out of five years of ownership and two out of five years of use don't have to be the same years.

Joint Filers Not Sharing a Residence

If you are living apart from your spouse and file jointly, each spouse can qualify for the $250,000 exclusion for their separate residences if they meet the ownership and use test.[9]

Example: Todd and Sarah are conducting a long-distance marriage. Todd has a home in California, while Sarah's home is in New York. If each owns and occupies his or her home for two of the last five years, they may each claim the $250,000 exclusion.

Once Every Two Years

The general rule is that you can use the exclusion once every two years. If you used the exclusion less than two years ago, you must wait until the two-year period has passed.[10] There are several exceptions to both the two-year ownership rule and the two-year use rule. These are discussed in Chapter 11.

Sandy's elaboration: Notice that you can use the exclusion every two years on different properties. This rule was not put into place for the average American, although it can benefit everyone. It was designed to benefit the wealthiest Americans. The reason is that many wealthy people own several homes. This way, they can sell their principal residence, avoid up to $500,000 of gain, move into their second home, and accomplish the same thing after living there for at least two years.

Recapture of Prior Depreciation Taken

This fantastic law allows you to avoid gain even if you rented out your home or used part of your home for business during the five-year period. However, you must recognize gain to the extent that you were allowed any depreciation taken after May 6, 1997.[11] Gain attributable to any post-May 6, 1997 depreciation will be taxed at your normal rate but up to a special long-term capital gain rate of 25 percent.[12] However, if you own the property less than 12 months, all depreciation is taxed at your ordinary income tax rate.

Example: Shari sold her home in 2006 with a $200,000 gain. She used her home as a home office and claimed depreciation on part of her home in prior years. If the depreciation taken was $10,000 after May 6, 1997, Shari must pay tax on the $10,000, taken at a maximum tax rate of 25 percent. She would be eligible to avoid the remaining gain under the exclusion. If, however, Shari held the property for less than 12 months, the recapture of depreciation would be at Shari's ordinary income tax rates. Ouch!

Home Handy-Man Relief Act

The universal exclusion also benefits folks who aren't rich. For example, it dramatically benefits people who are mechanically dexterous. They can buy a home in a good area, fix it up, live in it the required time, and sell it with little or no gain taxed. If you specialize in finding fixer-uppers, you can get rich.

Itinerant Landlord's Relief Act

If you rented out a home that has substantially appreciated, you would simply move into the rental home for two years. Upon sale, you would avoid most of the gain except for any depreciation taken. This can be a very nice loophole for you.

Example: Roy owns a home that he rents out and that has appreciated $230,000. Let's assume that he has taken $16,000 in depreciation over the last few years. If he sells the rental property, he will have to pay tax on the entire $230,000 of gain, which could be at the 15 percent capital gain rate and up to 25 percent on the gain attributable to the $16,000 of depreciation taken. Thus, he may have to pay $36,100 plus any state income tax. If Roy moves into the house for two years, he has to pay tax only on the depreciation taken. This would result in tax of only $4,000. He would save $32,100 in taxes. This would more than pay for the move plus the hassle of moving.

Hot tip: If spouses who file jointly move into a rental property, they can exclude up to $500,000 of gain and do this every two years with different properties!

Sandy's elaboration: I have a friend named Tony who bought newly constructed homes in Miami many years ago. When he first bought the homes and paid full price, I and others made fun of him. With the tremendous appreciation that has gone on in real estate, we aren't laughing now. I met Tony in Washington, DC, when he was working for the government. I suggested that he quit his job despite his statement that his government job was "the best paid unemployment around." I told him to kick out a tenant from one rental home and move into it for two years. After two years, he can sell the home and avoid up to $250,000 of gain. He should do this every two years for each rental property. His new job is kicking out tenants and moving into his rental homes. He now makes a lot more money than working at a job.

Election Out of Exclusion[13]

The exclusion rules automatically apply to your gain from your principal residence. However, you may elect out of the rules and pay tax on the gain. I know that you are wondering, "Why would anyone want to elect out of the exclusion and pay tax when they could have avoided it?" I'm glad you asked.

Normally they wouldn't want to pay the tax. However, there are circumstances where the rules are detrimental when you sell your home. For example, if you have two homes that were principal residences during different times within the past five years, and one has a substantial gain that has accrued over the years, you can sell the house with the smaller gain and then elect out of the rules. This way you can sell the house with the larger gain shortly thereafter and not be penalized by being able to use the rules every two years.

Example: Carmen has two homes that were used as principal residences within the past five years. House A has a slight appreciation of $50,000. House B has an appreciation of $240,000. If she sells house A and reports tax on the gain, she can then sell house B and use the full $250,000 exclusion against the gain from House B.

Summary

- If you are single, you can avoid up to $250,000 of gain on your principal residence. If you are married filing jointly, you can avoid up to $500,000 of gain on your principal residence.
- To use the full $500,000 exclusion, you or your spouse must have owned the principal residence for at least two of the prior five years, both you and your spouse must have occupied the principal residence for two of the prior five years, and neither spouse can have used the exclusion within the last two years.
- The ownership period and the occupancy period need not be the same.
- Joint filers living in different residences can each claim the $250,000 exclusion if they each meet the rules.
- The exclusion can be used once every two years. This means that you can avoid gain on your principal residence and then on any vacation home or second residence after you move into the second home for two years after the sale of the principal residence. This can also be used to avoid gain on rental property by moving into the property for two years and making it your principal residence.
- Don't forget that you have to recognize gain on any depreciation taken after May 6, 1977 at a maximum rate of 25 percent.
- Looking for fixer-uppers can make you wealthy. People who are very handy can move into them, fix them up, and live there for two years while they avoid up to $250,000 of gain or even $500,000 if married filing jointly and living together.

Notes

1 H.R. 2014, Congressional Committee Report Accompanying Taxpayer Relief Act of 1997, page 312

2 Section 121 (a) of the IRC

3 Section 121 (b)(2) of the IRC

4 Section 121(b)(2) of the IRC

5 Section 121 (b)(2) of the IRC

6 Section 121 (b)(1) of the IRC

7 Section 121 (b)(1) of the IRC and Rev. Rul. 80-172, 1980-2 CB 56

8 Section 121 (d)(6) of the IRC. By requiring depreciation recapture, Congress allows the home to be used for business or as a rental.

9 H.R. 2014, Congressional Committee Reports Accompanying Taxpayer Relief Act of 1997, page 312

10 Section 121 (b)(3)(a) of the IRC

11 Section 121 (b)(3)(a) of the IRC

12 Sections 1250 and 1 (h)(1)(D) of the IRC

13 Section 121(f) of the IRC

11

Exceptions to the Two-Year Rule

Another difference between death and taxes is that death is frequently painless.
—**Anonymous**

Overview
1. Learn how mental incapacity can override the two-year rule
2. Understand that changes in employment, health, and unforeseen circumstances can override the two-year requirements
3. Learn why you get a partial exclusion if you meet one of the exceptions to the rule

As you learned in Chapter 10, you must live and occupy your principal residence for two of the prior five years in order to fully use the Universal Exclusion. There are some exceptions to these two-year requirements even if you:

- Failed the two-year ownership requirement
- Failed the two-year use requirement[1]
- Used the exclusion within the last two years[2]

The key is that the primary reason for the sale or exchange is by reason of:[3]

1. Change in place of employment (you or your spouse)
2. Health, divorce, legal separation, joblessness, job change, change in self-employment, or multiple births
3. Other unforeseen circumstances

Sandy's elaboration: You can avoid the two-year requirements by reasons of health if you move to a new location to mitigate, diagnose, cure, or treat a disease, illness, or injury. You can't be moving simply because it is merely beneficial to your health. If you want to be safe regarding this exception, you should get a letter from a physician noting that you need to move for the above reasons.

Example: Murray was told to move to a warm climate by his doctor in order to alleviate his asthma. If he moves to Arizona after living in his principal residence for only one year, he may still use part of the exclusion. The two-year ownership and use requirements are waived.

Example: Karen was diagnosed with cancer. If she sells her home after living there for only one year in order to move to California to receive treatment from a specialized facility, the two-year ownership and use requirements are waived.

Example: Corey just took a job and purchased a new home three months ago. Sadly, he now loses his job. If he moves to a new location out of the city to obtain a new job, he may avoid the two-year ownership and use requirements even though he only lived in his home for three months.

Partial Exclusion for Hardship

As with much recent tax legislation, what Congress giveth, it taketh away. If any of the two-year requirements are waived, but you still don't meet one or more of the two-year rules, the amount of the exclusion is prorated by the lesser of the months that you met the rules divided by 24 months.[4]

Observation...

A partial exclusion is better than nothing!

Example: Sarah sells her home because she has a new job in another town. She has not used the exclusion in the last two years and has lived in her home for 12 months. Had she lived and occupied it for the full two years, she would be able to exclude up to $250,000 of gain. Because she met only half of the two-year rule by reason of her change in employment, she can avoid 50 percent of the potential $250,000 exclusion.

Sandy's elaboration: If Sarah didn't meet the hardship exception, she would have to pay tax on the whole gain. Even though she didn't get to use the entire $250,000 of exclusion, she may be able to avoid most of the gain anyway by being able to avoid $125,000 of gain in this instance. Getting a partial exclusion is certainly better than no exclusion!

Mental Incapacity Exception

Congress carved out an exception to the exception ... if you can believe it. There is one way you can avoid the two-year rule and get the full $250,000/$500,000, exclusion.

If a homeowner becomes physically or mentally incapable of self-care, he or she is deemed to meet the ownership and use requirements if he or she owned and used the home for only one year of the last five years.[5]

Example: Myra has been diagnosed with Alzheimer's disease. She lived in her home for one-and-a-half years before she needed to go to a nursing home for proper care. Despite the fact that she owned and used her residence for less than two years, she will be deemed to meet both the ownership and use requirements for the full $250,000 exclusion if her home is sold.

Other Unforeseen Circumstances

I have just outlined some of the situations in which you can get a partial or full exclusion even if you don't meet the two-year rules. These examples are not all-inclusive. Other reasons for the sale of your home that qualify as unforeseen circumstances would give rise to a partial exclusion. If you move due to a terrorist attack, act of war, or big fire, for example, these qualify as unforeseen circumstances. Another example involved a police officer who lived in a home less than two years and was required to move because of his neighbor's complaint that he kept a dog in his home as part of a K-9 unit and was prevented from constructing a kennel by his homeowners' association.[6] The bottom line is that if you must move because of unforeseen circumstances, you may be eligible for a partial exclusion.

Summary

- Although you need to occupy your home for two of the prior five years, you may obtain full exclusion if you sell your home because you become mentally incapable of self-care. Should this happen, you only need to meet the test for one of the prior five years.
- If you must move due to health, job loss, multiple births, divorce, legal separation, or other unforeseen circumstances, you may use part of the exclusion even if you failed to meet the two-year rules.
- The amount of the partial exclusion due to one of the exceptions noted above is equal to the lesser of the months that you meet the rules divided by 24 months.

Notes

1 Section 121 ©(2) of the IRC
2 Section 121 ©(2)(A) of the IRC
3 Section 121 ©(2)(B) of the IRC. See also 1.121-3 (d), and section 1.121-3(c) and 1.121- 3(e) of the Regs
4 Section 121 ©(1)(B) of the IRC
5 Section 121 (d)(7)(A) of the IRC
6 IRS Private Ruling 200504012

12

Divorce and Death Implications

Once—just once—I'd like to be fixed up with a guy who earns in a year what I pay in taxes.

—Anonymous female lawyer

Overview
1. Learn about the major tax trap that involves property transfers pursuant to a divorce
2. Understand a trap and a potential benefit that occurs upon the death of a spouse
3. Understand a major sales tip in finding and developing motivated sellers

Prior to 1997, there were a lot of tax traps if a home was transferred pursuant to a divorce. One trap noted that if you sold a home after several years of occupancy by the ex-spouse, you were not allowed to use the exclusion in effect at the time because you didn't personally occupy the home yourself. A second trap occurred if you sold the home to your spouse pursuant to a divorce. You were required to pay tax on the gain even if you didn't receive any cash. Even worse, this gain was treated as ordinary income rather than capital gain. Thus the selling spouse got a real shaft: tax without the cash to pay for it. The buying spouse made out very well because he or she got a step up in basis as if he or she had purchased a new home and didn't have to come up with any cash. Congress, therefore, tried to correct this problem for divorcing couples.[1]

Current Law

If you now transfer property incident to a divorce, any period of ownership during which the spouse or former spouse is granted use under the divorce or separation instrument counts as use by the transferring or selling spouse.[2]

71

Example: Jim and Sue are getting divorced. Pursuant to a judicial decree, Sue gets to live in the house until the divorce is final. Two years later, Jim sells his half-interest to a third party. Jim may now avoid up to $250,000 of gain because Sue's use counts as his use.

Major Divorce Problem

In order to avoid the potential tax that existed by transferring homes to the ex-spouse pursuant to a divorce, Congress changed the law and made it much more beneficial for the selling spouse to sell his or her interest in the home to his or her ex. The problem is that now the buying spouse gets a major shaft.

If you sell your home to your ex pursuant to a divorce decree, no gain or loss results to the transferring (selling) spouse.[3] Moreover, there is a carryover of the original basis in the home.[4] The original basis transfers to the buying spouse. After the transfer, your ex-spouse's basis is equal to the old joint basis. Gain or loss is measured against this basis.

Sandy's elaboration: Any payments made to buy the family home pursuant to a divorce do not increase or decrease the buying spouse's basis.[5] Thus the buying spouse gets no benefit from making any payments to buy out the ex-spouse's interest.

Example: Pursuant to a divorce decree, Marc sells his share of their home to his ex-spouse, Anita, for $400,000. If they originally paid $40,000 for the house 10 years ago, Anita's basis remains at $40,000. She gets no benefit from the $460,000 payment or settlement. Yuck!

Sales tip: In a divorce involving a family house that has substantially appreciated, realtors should inform the couple of this nasty surprise and recommend that the family home be sold to a third party. Each spouse can then buy a new home with the tax-free money that they get, and the realtor gets three deals: the sale of the old home and the purchase of the new home for each spouse. Three deals are better than one!

Sandy's elaboration: This chapter assumes that you got your home pursuant to a divorce or death of a spouse who was joint owner. If you inherited a home from someone who wasn't a joint owner with you, then the new basis becomes the fair market value as of the date of death.

Property of a Deceased Spouse

If you are now unmarried but you were married and your spouse died, Congress allows a benefit for you. The ownership and use requirements include the period that the deceased spouse owned and used the property even if the surviving spouse is not living there currently.[6]

Sandy's elaboration: Most homes are owned jointly with a spouse. If you live in a state that is not a community property state and your spouse dies, you receive a step up in basis for the spouse's half-interest.[7] If you and your spouse paid $40,000 for your home that is worth $600,000 at the time of the death of your spouse, your basis in the home becomes $320,000—one-half of your original basis plus one-half of the fair market value of the home at the time of your spouse's death. Essentially, you inherit the fair market value of your spouse's interest at the time of your spouse's death.

Observation: You are allowed to file a joint return in the year of your spouse's death. If your home is sold during the year that a joint return is filed, you may be able to exclude up to $500,000 of gain if:

1. Either spouse satisfied the ownership test
2. Both spouses satisfied the use test
3. Neither spouse used the exclusion within the last two years

Sandy's elaboration: Even with the partial step up in basis for your spouse's interest, if the appreciation is more than your total basis and you sell the home in the year of death, you can avoid up to $500,000 of gain. If the gain is less than $250,000 above the new adjusted basis, then you can wait to sell the home because you will get your own $250,000 of basis.

A Surviving Spouse Can Wait Two Years after the Year of Death

In addition to being able to claim the full $500,000 for sale in the year of death, you may file a joint return as a surviving spouse[8] for two years after the year of death of your spouse and therefore exclude up to $500,000 of appreciation, including postdeath appreciation, if:

1. Your spouse died within the two preceding tax years of the current year of sale
2. You maintained a household (which means you provided over half the cost of the household[9]) as a principal place of abode for your dependent son, stepson, daughter, or stepdaughter,[10] or for adopted children.[11]
3. You haven't remarried before the close of the tax year in which you want to file a joint return[12]
4. You must have been able to file a joint return with your deceased spouse.[13] If you were divorced from your deceased ex-spouse, you cannot file jointly in either the year of death or thereafter.[14]

Example: Heather's husband died last year. They lived in the home for many years and neither spouse used the exclusion within the last two years. After her husband's death, she moved into another home with her dependent son. If she were to sell the home, she would qualify for the

Checking Obituaries

$500,000 exclusion because the use and ownership requirements were met and she can file a joint return as a surviving spouse.

Sales tip: If you are a realtor and find yourself in a situation where there is a surviving spouse who has a residence that has appreciated more than $250,000 above the new basis (which, if previously owned jointly with a deceased owner, is half the original basis plus the fair market value of the deceased owner's one-half interest), the surviving spouse needs to know that he or she must sell the home within two years of the spouse's death to be able to file jointly and use up to $500,000 of the exclusion. Otherwise, the exclusion is limited to $250,000. If a person has a deceased spouse but no dependent children living with him, he may not qualify as a surviving spouse. This means that he or she can file jointly only in the taxable year of death of the spouse and use the $500,000 exclusion only in that year.

Observation: Although it may sound ghoulish, reading the obituaries becomes even more vital today than it ever was, especially for areas that have had great appreciation. As a realtor you may be doing your clients a tremendous favor by informing them of this rule, and you can certainly get a sense of urgency to sell as a result.

Community Property State

Everything said above applies to states that are not community property states. If you own your home jointly in a community property state, you get a different result. Community property states are: Arizona, California, Idaho, Louisiana, Nevada, New Mexico, Texas, state of Washington, and Wisconsin. Alaska has an election to be covered under community property rules.

All property held jointly would get a step up in basis to the fair market value as of the date of death of the deceased spouse.[15] Any property that was deemed separate property (property bought before you were married and titled in your name) does not get a step up in basis.[16]

Example: Donnie and Marie live in the community property state of Nevada. They paid $100,000 for their jointly owned home that is now worth $1,000,000. If Donnie died, Marie's basis would be the fair market value of $1,000,000. Had they lived in a non–community-property state, her basis would have been $550,000 (half of the original cost plus half of the fair market value at the date of Donnie's death).

Summary

- If the transfer or sale of a house is made incident to a divorce, any period of ownership and occupancy during which the spouse or former spouse is granted use under the divorce instrument also counts as use by the transferred or selling spouse.
- Sale of a home to your ex pursuant to a divorce produces a trap. The buying spouse's basis is equal to the old joint basis and measures gain or loss against that basis. Cash payments made by the buying spouse produce no benefit or increase in basis. Yuck! In a divorce situation, it is much better to sell the family home to a third party than to one of the spouses.
- Property that was owned jointly and received by the surviving spouse or joint owner gets a partial basis increase. The new basis equals half of the old basis plus the fair market value of the deceased owner's half-interest. If there are only two owners, this translates to half of the original basis plus half of the fair market value at the date of death of the joint owner.
- If you were able to file a joint return with your deceased spouse, you may claim the full $500,000 exclusion if the house is sold in the year of death of the deceased owner. This will be a benefit only if the house has appreciated more than $250,000 from the new adjusted basis.

- If you qualify as a surviving spouse, you can get the full $500,000 exclusion if the house is sold within the two succeeding tax years after the year of death of your spouse.
- If you live in a community property state, you get a full step up in basis for jointly held property by spouses. This is a different result than that found in non–community–property states.

Notes

1 H.R. 2014, Congressional Committee Report Accompanying Taxpayer Relief Act of 1997, page 312
2 Section 121 (d)(3)(B) of the IRC
3 Section 1041(a) of the IRC
4 Section 1041(b) of the IRC
5 *Ibid*
6 Section 121(d)(2) of the IRC
7 Sections 1014(a), 2040(b)(1), and 1014 (b)(9) of the IRC. See also instructions on IRS Form 706, part 5.
8 Section 2(a)(1) of the IRC
9 Section 2(a)(1)(B)(i) of the IRC
10 Section 2(a)(1)B)(ii) of the IRC
11 Section 1.2-2(a)(1)(ii) of the Regs
12 Section 1.2-2(a)(1)(i) of the Regs
13 Section 2(a)(2)(B) of the IRC
14 Section 1.2-2(a)(4) of the Regs
15 Section 1014(b)(6) of the IRC and 1.1014-2(a)(5) of the Regs
16 *Crosby vs. Comm.*, T.C. Memo 1961-272

13

Using an S Corporation to Avoid the Two-Year Rule

You first have to decide whether to use the short or the long form. The short form is what the Internal Revenue Service calls "simplified," which means it is designed for people who need the help of a Sears tax preparation expert to distinguish between their first and last names. The IRS wants you to use the short form because it gets to keep most of your money. So unless you have pond silt for brains, you want the long form.

—Unknown

Overview
1. Learn how to beat the two-out-of-five-year exclusionary rule using an S Corporation
2. Understand how using an S Corporation can get you a huge increase in depreciation over simply renting out your home
3. Learn how to avoid the most important trap in selling to your S Corporation

As you learned in Chapter 10, you can avoid up to $250,000 gain if single or $500,000 if married filing jointly if you own and occupy your principal residence for two of the prior five years.

What happens if you have met the ownership requirement of your home but have rented it out for seven years? If you rent out the home for more than three of the prior five years, you will not have used the home as a residence for the required two out of five years and will not be eligible for any exclusion.

If you decide to rent out your home, your basis for depreciation is the lower of your original adjusted basis and the fair market value.[1] This means that if property is appreciating, your basis for depreciation will be your adjusted basis, not the current fair market value.

Example: Marvin and Gayle bought a home for $50,000 many years ago. Today their home is worth $500,000. If they were to rent it out, their basis for depreciation would be the original cost basis of $50,000.

Sell to Your S Corporation

A possible solution that can be used to avoid both of the above problems is to sell your home to your 100 percent owned S corporation. According to the IRS, there is no ban on the sale of your home to your 100 percent owned corporation.[2] In other words, the sale of your home to your corporation should be a valid sale for purposes of the exclusionary rule.

Why an S Corporation?

With an S corporation, the gain from a sale flows to your personal tax return and is subject to only one level of tax.[3] With a regular corporation, you face double taxation on gains. At what price must you sell to your corporation? There is only one acceptable price—you must sell at fair market value.

Corporation's Basis in Your Home

Your corporation's basis in the home is equal to the price paid and costs of closing the transaction. Selling your home to your S corporation can substantially increase your basis for gain and loss and for depreciation.

Example: Let's use the example with Marvin and Gayle noted above. They paid $50,000 for a home that is now worth $500,000. If they simply rent out the home, their basis for depreciation becomes $50,000. If, however, they sell their home to their S corporation for the full $500,000, which in turn rents out the home, the corporation's basis for depreciation is now $500,000. Marvin and Gayle, through their corporation, get a tenfold increase in depreciation over what they would have gotten had they simply rented out the house. If they were coming to the end of the two-year exclusionary rule, they would use this sale to meet the rule.

Caution: You, as the S corporation owner, will have to fund the corporation's purchase with sufficient cash to take advantage of any annual losses because you must have sufficient basis in your S corporation stock to at least equal any loss pass-through.[4] The amount of the loss you use reduces your S corporation stock basis.

Example: Debra has a loss in her S corporation of $6,321, which occurred from renting out the property and taking depreciation. Her basis in her S corporation is zero because she deducted pass-through losses from prior years. She must contribute cash of at least $6,321 to her S corporation to have the loss pass through to her individual tax return. Cash contributions increase your basis in the stock.[5]

Sandy's elaboration: One question that I get is "How does the corporation get the cash to buy my home?" You simply need to contribute enough cash for the corporation to give you a down payment. You would fund the rest of the purchase by taking back a note. If the house is worth $400,000, you might give the corporation $20,000 in cash to fund the down payment and closing costs and take a note for the remaining $380,000 at 5 percent interest. Your corporation could then either rent out the house or sell it.

Ordinary Income on Sale to the Corporation

A sale to your S corporation is only advised to be accomplished with your *principal residence* and *only if your appreciation is approximately equal to or less than the exclusionary amount.* The reason for this caution is that any gain not covered by the exclusion is taxed at ordinary income tax rates rather than capital gains rates.[6] However, if you sell your principal residence to the S corporation, where the gain is less than the exclusion, you don't pay any tax on the income under the exclusionary rule. Under this rule, you avoid $250,000 of gain ($500,000 if married filing jointly) if you meet the criteria. In addition, this exclusion results in a permanent exclusion, not just a deferral.

Example: Martin sells his principal residence to his S corporation after owning and occupying the house for two of the prior five years. His total gain is $240,000. This would be taxed at ordinary income rates; however, he pays no tax due to the exclusionary rule.

Example: Martin accidentally sells the wrong property, his rental property, which has appreciated the same $240,000, to his S corporation. The whole $240,000 gain is taxed at ordinary income tax rates. Yuck!

Meet the Two-Year Test with a Legitimate Sale to Relatives

If you don't want to use the S corporation technique but must sell your home quickly in order to meet the requirements for the exclusionary rule because time is getting short, consider a sale to certain relatives. Perhaps mom or dad or your brother or sister would buy your home and then resell it. You could take back a first or second mortgage to ensure a speedy transaction. If you make a bona fide sale to them, and they buy it to either use it as a home or to make a profit, you get the exclusion and they get the title to the home.

Advantages

Unlike a sale to your S corporation that turns capital gain into ordinary income (absent the exclusion), you treat the gain on the sale to a relative as if you made the sale to someone unrelated to you. All gains on sales made to parents or siblings are capital gains, which can be eliminated using the exclusion.

Move Back into the Rental Property

If time is getting short, and you need to sell the property quickly in order to meet the exclusionary rule time limits, you might want to move back into the property for two years and rent it out for less than three years.

Summary

- If time is getting short for you to meet the exclusionary time rules, consider selling your principal residence to your S corporation. This will allow you to meet the two-year rules, and you can avoid up to $250,000 of gain if single or $500,000 of gain if married filing jointly.
- Don't sell your second home, vacation home, or your rental property to your S corporation because all gain would be taxed at ordinary income rates.
- Don't sell your principal residence to your S corporation if the appreciation substantially exceeds the exclusionary limits.

- If time is short, consider selling your principal residence to your parents or siblings.
- If time is getting short, consider moving back into the home and living there for two years, which will restart the time test for the exclusionary rule.

Notes

1 Section 1012 of the IRC and sections 1.165-9(b)(2) and 1.167-(g)(1) of the Regs
2 P.L.R. 8350084
3 Section 1366 of the IRC
4 Section 1366(d)(1) of the IRC
5 Sections 1366 and 1367 of the IRC. See also *DeJoy vs. Commissioner*, T.C. Memo 2000-162
6 Section 1239 of the IRC

Part 4

Introduction to Tax Planning for Buying and Looking for Rental Property

In this part you will learn about computing depreciation and why depreciation is the one of the best U.S. government giveaways. You will also learn to evaluate your return on investment for almost any real property and how you can write off the cost of looking for property.

14

Introduction to Investment Property

Only the little people pay taxes.
—Attributed to hotel magnate Leona Helmsley

Overview

1. Understand why rental property gives even greater tax benefits than owning a home
2. Understand tax planning for buying, owning, and disposing of rental property
3. Learn when to and when not to give seller financing

This chapter gives you an overview of what is discussed in the next two parts dealing with rental investments.

What is most interesting about rental property is that it is your best tax-sheltered investment; rental property, can be an even better tax shelter than your home. Why? Home ownership produces great tax benefits, but the benefits multiply for rental property! Not only do you get the same opportunity for leverage and appreciation in value, but also you get great tax deductions while you own the investment. As with home ownership, you must be aware of the tax implications of rental property ownership for the following:

1. When you buy rental property: As with the purchase of your home, you must make sure that your records and tax strategy establish your initial tax basis. In addition, you might be able to get tax breaks when you look for rental properties.
2. While you own rental property: There is more good news. In addition to mortgage interest and real estate taxes, you get many more tax deductions. The best of all is depreciation. However, look out for Uncle Sam's devious efforts to limit your goodies, such as with the passive loss rules

and vacation home limitations. We also discuss some of the amazing income-shifting opportunities where you can get a deduction equivalent to the cost of your kid's college or wedding.

3. When you dispose of rental property: Here is the best news of all. You can use Uncle Sam as a banker for you to pyramid into bigger and better investment real estate via a tax-deferred exchange.

4. When to allow seller financing: If you are willing to finance the purchase of either a home or investment property, installment reporting can give you a big economic advantage for several reasons. You get to spread the tax over many years and have the untaxed portion of the note making interest for you, and you get positive cash flow with negative taxable income at the same time. This tax loss can save tax dollars by offsetting it against other income. In effect, you get paid and the government only gets the leftovers.

Sandy's elaboration: The discussion of rental property is more complicated than the discussion about your home. This is true because Congress decided to put a few tax traps along the way to limit the benefits. The good news is that we show you how to avoid most of those traps so you can get all those wonderful tax-sheltered benefits. The following material will increase your rate of return on rental property investments significantly each year.

Concepts You Should Know for Future Chapters

Based on prior chapters, there are certain topics that you need to remember and understand before we delve into the rental property chapters.

Computation of Basis

Basis is used to determine gain and loss. If you sell your property for more than your basis, you have a gain. If you sell for less than your basis, you have a loss. The formula for basis is cost + improvements – depreciation = basis.

Sandy's elaboration: The key element is that depreciation always reduces your basis. If you inherit property, your basis is fair market value of the decedent's interest at death. If you owned property jointly with your spouse in a non-community-property state, your basis is the fair market value of the decedent's interest plus your share of the cost. If you live in a community property state and inherit property that you own jointly with your spouse, your basis is fair market value.

Example: Arlene paid $300,000 for a rental investment and took $10,000 in depreciation before she sold the property. Her basis for both gain and loss is $290,000 (cost less depreciation).

Computation of Gain or Loss

Gain is selling price minus basis. If the selling price is less than your basis, you have a loss.

Example: Anita has a basis in her real estate of $400,000. If she sells her property for $500,000, her gain is $100,000.

Computation of Tax on Gain

Tax on gain derived from investment real estate isn't as easy to compute as it should be. There are separate rules for figuring tax rates on depreciation. You claim long-term capital gain on the remaining part of the gain. For depreciation taken, you pay tax at the lower of your normal tax rate or 25 percent, whichever is less. We assume throughout this book that you pay tax on depreciation taken at the maximum rate of 25 percent. Any gain above depreciation depends on your tax bracket. Long-term capital gain, which deals with property held over a year, is taxed at a maximum federal rate of 15 percent plus your state rate. If your normal tax rate is 10 to 15 percent, the long-term rate drops to only 5 percent. We assume that you pay 15 percent tax on your long-term capital gain and that your state tax rate is 6 percent. This may be more or less than your state's tax rate, in which case you will have to make allowances accordingly.

Summary

- Basis is used in determining gain or loss.
- If you sell property for more than your adjusted basis, you have a gain. If you sell property for less than your adjusted basis, you have a loss. Losses on principal residences are generally not deductible, while losses on rental or commercial property are deductible.
- Basis begins with cost. Add improvements and subtract depreciation.
- If you inherit property, basis is fair market value at the time of the decedent's death. If property is owned jointly in non-community-property states, basis is half of fair market value plus your share of cost in the property. In community property states, basis of inherited jointly owned property is fair market value.
- Tax on depreciation is the lower of your normal tax rate or 25 percent.
- If you hold real estate for at least one year, you are eligible for long-term capital gains rates.

15

Understanding Depreciation

We have a tax code that favors those with the best accountants.

—Shane Keats

Overview
1. Understand why depreciation is a huge gift from the government
2. Learn when you can start depreciating your property
3. Learn how to compute depreciation for any investment real estate

One of the most exciting tax benefits for rental property is the deduction for depreciation. Even if your property is appreciating in value, you are still allowed to deduct depreciation.[1] Thus, you get a tax deduction with no concurrent cash or economic outlay. It is like a gift from Uncle Sam. Does this seem too good to be true? It is, sort of. You must also reduce your basis to calculate gain from sale.[2]

Example: Mike and Susan own some rental property whose cost basis is $400,000. If they depreciate their property by $20,000 before they sell it, their new basis for both gain and loss becomes $380,000, which is the original cost less depreciation.

Any gain on the property will be taxed at the lower of their normal tax rate up to a maximum of 25 percent or depreciation that they have taken on the property.[3] The balance is long-term capital gain, subject to a special maximum rate of 15 percent. This is reduced to 5 percent if you are in the 10 percent or 15 percent bracket on ordinary income.

Sandy's elaboration: This is still a good deal because your tax on other types of income, such as compensation or interest, can be as high as 35 percent.

Example: Becky and her significant other own some rental property for which they paid $300,000. They took $10,000 in depreciation deduction, giving them a $290,000 basis. If they sell the property for $400,000, they will pay tax computed as follows:

$$25\% \times \$10,000 = \$2,500$$

$$15\% \times \$100,000 = \$15,000$$

$$8\% \text{ (state rate)} \times \$110,000^4 = \$8,800$$

Total tax: $26,300

Benefits of Turning Depreciation into Capital Gain

Most people never realize how beneficial depreciation really is. Depreciation alone can make you a nice profit even if the property never appreciates. This is illustrated by the following example.

Example: Let's assume you buy rental property for $150,000 and sell it years later for the same price. Let's also assume that you took $50,000 in depreciation. Ignoring the time value of money, your federal tax benefit would look like this:

Depreciation deductions claimed: $50,000
Federal tax benefit rate: 35 percent
Tax refund: $17,500
Selling price of the property: $150,000
Basis ($150,000 – $50,000): $100,000
Gain on sale: $50,000
Federal tax rate on depreciation: 25 percent
Tax paid on sale of property: $12,500
Tax benefit from depreciation: $5,000

Sandy's elaboration: As you can see, when depreciation turns into capital gains, you come out ahead even if you don't sell the property at a profit. This is one of the most amazing aspects about real estate.

When to Start Depreciating Property

One question I often get at seminars is "When can I start depreciating my property?" The answer is that you start depreciating your property and start deducting repairs when the house is available for rent.[5]

Example: In January, Mario buys a property that needs a lot of repairs. He finishes fixing up the property in June. He places an ad in the paper on July 1 and a tenant moves in on September 1. Mario may start depreciating the property beginning on July 1, when the property was available for rent. He does not have to wait until September 1, the date the tenant took occupancy.

How to Figure Depreciation

If you look at Figure 15-1, you will see two depreciation schedules: one for residential rental property and one for commercial property. Residential property has more favorable rates in that you write off your property over 27.5 years using the straight-line method. Commercial real estate is written off over 39 years using the straight-line method. Thus, the question is whether your property falls into the residential or commercial category.

Normally, most people can tell which category applies. If you have an apartment house or other location where people live, you come within the residential category. If you have a storefront or commercial office building, the commercial category applies. Sometimes, however, this gets a bit muddled.

Depreciation

**Post-1986 Recovery Percentages
for Residential Rental Property (27.5 years)**

Year	Month of Recovery Year											
	1	2	3	4	5	6	7	8	9	10	11	12
1	3.485	3.182	2.879	2.576	2.273	1.970	1.667	1.364	1.061	0.758	0.455	0.152
2–18	3.636	3.636	3.636	3.636	3.636	3.636	3.636	3.636	3.636	3.636	3.636	3.636
19–27	3.637	3.637	3.637	3.637	3.637	3.637	3.637	3.637	3.637	3.637	3.637	3.637
28	1.970	2.273	2.576	2.879	3.182	3.485	3.636	3.636	3.636	3.636	3.636	3.636
29	0.000	0.000	0.000	0.000	0.000	0.000	0.152	0.455	0.758	1.061	1.364	1.667

**Post-May 23, 1993 Recovery Percentages
for Nonresidential Rental Property (40 years)**

Year	Month of Recovery Year											
	1	2	3	4	5	6	7	8	9	10	11	12
1	2.461	2.247	2.033	1.819	1.605	1.391	1.177	0.963	0.749	0.535	0.321	0.107
2–39	2.564	2.564	2.564	2.564	2.564	2.564	2.564	2.564	2.564	2.564	2.564	2.564
40	0.107	0.321	0.535	0.749	0.963	1.177	1.391	1.605	1.189	2.033	2.247	2.461

Figure 15-1

For example, you might have residential apartments located on top of a storefront. Congress thought of this situation.

Residential property is defined as "any property where 80 percent or more of the gross receipts are from rental of dwelling units."[6] A dwelling unit is a house or apartment used to provide living accommodations, but is not a hotel, motel, or other establishment in which more than 50 percent of the units are used on a transient basis.[7]

Sandy's elaboration: If less than 80 percent of the gross receipts are from residential rentals, the entire building is deemed to be commercial property.

Example: Shelby owns a mini strip mall with some apartments located on top of the stores. He receives $20,000 a month in rent, of which $8,000 is from the apartments. The building is considered commercial property because less than 80 percent of the gross rent is from residential dwelling units.

Once you know which category your property falls in, you go to the Figure 15-1 correct table in Figure 15-1 and Appendix 3 and find the beginning month of depreciation, which is at the top of the table. You choose the column corresponding to the month that you placed the property into service and follow the column each year thereafter. Each number represents the percentage of the purchase price that is allocated to the building, which will represent that year's depreciation.

Example: Jim and Sue place a residential property with a depreciable basis of $100,000 into service on July 10 of the current year. To calculate this year's depreciation, use column 7 (representing the seventh month) of the residential property table. Multiply the depreciable tax basis by 1.667 percent, which yields a depreciation deduction of $1,667 ($100,000 × 1.667%). Next year, multiply the same depreciable basis by $3.636 percent, yielding a deduction of $3,636 (3.636 × $100,000), and so on for the following years.

Example: Jim and Sue buy a storefront for $100,000 in April. This is commercial property, so the commercial property tables are used. Their depreciation for the first three years is as follows:

Year 1: $1,819 ($100,000 × 1.819%)
Yeas 2–39: $2,564 per year ($100,000 × 2.934%)
Year 40: $535

The Alternative Minimum Tax (AMT) Strikes Again

If you are subject to AMT, things don't look as good. The AMT requires you to use the alternative depreciation system, which is calculated using a 40-year straight-line rate for both residential and commercial property.

This will not yield as high a deduction as the regular 27.5 years for residential property.

Summary

- Depreciation is a great gift from Uncle Sam because it requires no cash outlay.
- You have to reduce your basis by depreciation.
- You are taxed on gain from the sale of real estate held for over one year at a maximum rate of 15 percent long-term capital gain rate.
- People in the 10 to 15 percent ordinary income tax bracket are taxed at a long-term capital gain rate of 5 percent.
- Gain attributable to depreciation is taxed at a special maximum rate of 15 percent.
- Depreciation begins when the property is available for rent.
- Residential and commercial property depreciation schedules are also found in Appendix 3. They use a percentage of the sale price based on the month that the property was placed in service.
- Residential property rates apply when 80 percent or more of the gross rental income is from the rent of dwelling units.
- Hotels or motels that cater to people on a transient basis are considered commercial property.

Notes

1 Section 167 for property placed in service before 1981. Section 168 for property placed in service thereafter.
2 Section 1016(a)(1) of the IRC
3 Sections 1250 and 1(h)(1)(D) and 1(h)(6) of the IRC. I should note that for most people, depreciation will be taxed at a maximum rate of 25 percent. This is the rate that I use when figuring out my possible return on investment. Any gain on sale beyond the depreciation taken is generally taxed at a flat rate of 15 percent for long-term capital gains plus any state rate.
4 This is taxed at the whole gain over basis because many states don't have a favorable rate for just depreciation.
5 Section 1.167(a)-11(e)(1)(i) of the Regs. See also Rev. Rul. 76-238, 1976-1 C.B. 55. See also *Simonson vs. U.S.* 7752 F.2d 341 (8th Cir. 1985).
6 Section 168(3)(2)(A)(i) of the IRC
7 Section 168(e)(2)(A)(ii) of the IRC

16

How to Evaluate Rates of Return for Residential Investment Property

An economy breathes through its tax loopholes.

—Barry Bracewell-Milnes

Overview
1. Understand how to figure rates of return for rental properties
2. Learn how to use the calculation sheet, which will work for any real estate investment

I think the best way to explain how to analyze the rental property decision is to use an example. There is a lot of real estate investment data available from realtors who specialize in investment properties. When you buy a property, you will be given the following information:

1. Rental income: This is determined by comparables.
2. Mortgage interest: This is the current interest rate. Banks will quote you the current rate, and it is usually found in the local Sunday newspaper.
3. Property taxes: These can be gleaned from the property records or you can ask a realtor who specializes in investment property.
4. Yearly repairs: I usually estimate 3 to 5 percent of the rental income depending on the age of the property.
5. Insurance: You can get this from an investment realtor or an insurance company. Typically, insurance is about 0.4 percent of the fair market value of the property.
6. Depreciation: This is computed using the chart in Appendix 3.

7. Tax rate for rental property losses: This is the benefit you receive on your tax return from generating real estate losses.

8. Mortgage principal for the first few years: You can get this by using an amortization calculator, asking a realtor who is familiar with investments, or purchasing amortization tables.

9. Property management: You can ask a property manager in your area what he charges. Normal charges are between 6 to 8 percent of rental income.

10. Vacancy: Many people forget to filter in a vacancy factor. No matter how well meaning you are or how wonderful your properties are, a vacancy will occur from time to time. I use one month per year for a vacancy factor. This means that 8.3 percent of your rent should be charged off under vacancy. Don't forget this because it will happen.

11. Tax on sale: This is the federal and state tax you pay if you sell the property. Federal tax is usually 25 percent of depreciation plus 15 percent of gain above depreciation. In addition, you add the state tax rate. All gain must be reduced by commissions paid to realtors and for closing costs.

 Sandy's elaboration: If you want, this is one chapter that can be skipped by you since I would strongly urge you to evaluate gain and tax on rental properties using the real estate software available. Figuring out gain and tax by hand is very cumbersome and only suitable for the bravest accountants and planners. This type of software can be found on the Web, such as in my links section of www.taxreductioninstitute.com or at various investment conventions. However, understanding this material will make the software more understandable and give you better insight into figuring out your return on investment. Don't forget that with software, garbage in equals garbage out!

Example: Joseph and Mary purchased a rental property for $280,000. They are now selling it for $350,000 after previously taking $12,000 in depreciation. Their tax on the sale is computed as follows:

- 25 percent of the depreciation plus
- 15 percent on the appreciation plus
- State tax (8 percent in this example) on both the depreciation and gain
- Total tax = $20,060

Example: Snow White is considering buying a rental property for $200,000 and holding it for one year. What would her after-tax rate of return be if she makes a down payment of 15 percent? Assume she is in the 30 percent income tax bracket—federal and state combined. Assume that there is an existing tenant, which means zero vacancy for this year. Assume that the mortgage principal for the first year is $1,000. Also assume that the property appreciates $21,000, but she negotiates commissions approximating $11,000; thus, the net appreciation is $10,000.

Rental income:	$19,200
Mortgage interest:	$11,000
Property taxes:	$1,400
Estimated repairs:	$900
Management fees:	$1,200
Insurance:	$300
Depreciation[1]:	$6,970
Total expenses:	$21,770

We will also assume that her taxes on the sale were $3,985.[2]
A. Gross amount realized:

Sale price:	$221,000
Less commissions and closing costs:	$11,000
Less basis:	$193,030
Cost:	$200,000
Less depreciation:	$6,970
Net gain:	$16,970[3]

Sandy's elaboration: Depreciation always reduces your basis.
B. Tax computation on sale of the property:

25 percent of depreciation[4]:	$1,742
15 percent capital gains rate on appreciation:	$1,500
8 percent state tax rate on whole gain above basis:	$1,358
Total tax on sale:	$4,600

Solved Example

Step 1: Tax Loss

Rental income for year	$19,200
Mortgage interest	$(11,000)
Property taxes	$(1,400)
Repairs	$(900)
Property management fee	$(1,200)
Insurance	$(300)
Depreciation	$(6,970)
Tax Loss	$($2,570)

Step 2: Tax Refund

Tax loss	($2,570)
Times tax rate	× .30
Tax refund	$771

Step 3: Cash Flow

Rental income	$19,200
Tax refund	$771
Mortgage interest	($11,000)
Mortgage principal	(1,000)
Property taxes	(1,400)
Repairs	(900)
Management fees	(1,200)
Insurance	$(300)
Net cash flow	$4,171

Step 4: Profit (Loss)

Cash flow	$4,171
Appreciation	$10,000
Tax on sale	($4,600)
Net profit	$9,571
Divided by cash investment	$30,000
Net return on investment	31.9%

 Sandy's elaboration: Although figuring your return on investment is not normally part of a tax course, I felt this would be useful for your evaluation of potential investments. This form is found in Appendix 2—I waived copyright, so feel free to use it. When you see items in parentheses, this means you subtract that number from the total.

Whew, this was a complicated chapter. However, if you understand how gain and tax are computed, it will greatly enable you to understand how to use the real estate software available to you. Such software is readily found on the Web or at investment conventions.

Summary

- Compute the tax on real estate investments as follows:

    1. 15% on the appreciation (which is the sale price minus your cost plus improvements) plus,

2. 25% on the depreciation (assuming you are in the 25% tax bracket or higher, otherwise use your actual tax bracket)

- The state rate times the total gain (sale price minus basis). This can also be figured by multiplying the state rate times the appreciation plus the depreciation previously taken.
- Don't forget to take at least a one-month vacancy into account.

Notes

1 We assumed that the property was purchased in January of the year. If you go to Appendix 2 and check out the residential rates, you will see the factor of 3.485 per 100 dollars of sale price. Thus, a sale price of $200,000 would result in depreciation of $6,970 (3.485 times 2,000).

2 This was computed by taking 25 percent of the depreciation of $6,970 plus a capital gains rate of 15 percent of the excess plus a state tax rate of 8 percent for a total tax of $3,985. Federal tax law requires you to pay tax on depreciation at the lower of your normal rate or 25 percent. It is easier to simply use the 25 percent.

3 Net gain is always sale price less commissions and closing cost less adjusted basis. Don't forget that depreciation always reduces basis.

4 You would pay tax on depreciation of the lower of your normal federal rate or 25 percent. Usually it is easier and more correct to use 25 percent as the tax rate on depreciation.

17

How to Deduct the Cost of Looking for Property

Don't tax you. Don't tax me. Tax the companies across the sea.
—Dan Rostenkowski, commenting on what people want from tax reform

Overview
You may incur four types of costs when you look for rental property:
1. Capital costs, which you add to the basis of the property and then allocate to the land and building
2. Costs that are deductible as expenses for business expansion
3. Nondeductible investigatory costs that are deemed personal in nature
4. Start-up costs for a business

People often ask me how they can deduct the cost of looking for real estate investment properties. It seems to be a huge concern that has not been addressed correctly in any book I have seen.

The good news for you is we authoritatively answer the question. The bad news is that several years ago, Congress enacted tax simplification in this area, which really means they muddied the works and made things more complicated.

Costs to Buy Your First Rental Property

Unless you are expanding your business to locations where rental property already exists, in order to deduct the cost of investigatory trips, you must target a specific property for investigation before you trigger identification of costs that produce tax benefits. With no target in mind, the cost of looking into the acquisition of your first rental property is generally personal and nondeductible. Once you identify a property you want to purchase, you may incur expenses to investigate and purchase the property, including costs for:

- Entertainment expenses
- Travel expenses
- Automobile expenses
- Appraisal fees
- Accounting fees
- Legal fees

You include the above costs as part of the property's tax basis.[1] You then allocate the tax basis to the land, building, and equipment as part of the purchase price to calculate your depreciation deductions.[2]

When the Targeted Purchase Fails

If acquisition of the targeted property fails, you may be able to deduct the costs expended in attempting to purchase the rental property.[3]

Sandy's elaboration: Note the key words "targeted" and "acquisition." Your travel expenses incurred to buy a rental property must be more than investigatory; they must be to acquire a specific rental property.[4] You benefit from any costs expended to buy a targeted rental property. Investigatory expenses incurred to buy personal property such as your home or second home are not deductible or amortizable. We are only talking about costs incurred to buy investment real estate.

Exception

Despite what was said about targeting a specific rental property, you may deduct investigatory expenses for looking at possible rental property purchases if you are trying to expand your existing business and you own a rental property in the location where you are looking. To write off investigatory expenses without targeting a specific property, you must:

1. Be in the business of renting real estate, which means owning at least six rental properties
2. Expend money to expand your holdings with similar property[5]
3. Expand in the area where you already own rental property[6]

What Is a Rental Business?

In the famous Curphey case, the tax court held that owning six properties such as two townhouses, three condominium units, and one single family house qualified as a rental business, which allowed him a home office deduction.[7]

It appears that owning at least six rental units, even if they are in fewer than six properties, may qualify for a rental business. In the case of *Fairey vs. Comm.*, Fairey owned 21 rental units housed in five properties. The tax court ruled that Fairey was in the business of renting real estate.[8]

Sandy's elaboration: If you want to deduct investigatory travel expenses without targeting a specific property, you must have a minimum of six rental units and at least one property in the area where you are looking.

Example: Sam owns two duplexes and two single-family homes that he rents out in the Washington DC area. If he looks for new property near Washington DC, his travel expenses are deductible.

Example: Assume Sam owns three duplexes in Washington DC and three in Indianapolis and he looks for more property in Indianapolis. His travel expenses incurred while looking for property in Indianapolis are deductible because he owns at least six rental units and has at least one rental unit where he is looking for more property.

Example: Assume Sam owns the same properties in Washington DC and in Indianapolis but decides to look for property in Tulsa. He may not deduct the cost of looking for property unless he targets a specific property for purchase and the targeted purchase doesn't occur. The reason is because he doesn't already own a rental unit in Tulsa.

What Happens If You Buy the Targeted Property?

If you buy the targeted property, the tax consequences differ as to whether you have an active rental property business. See Figure 17-1, the flowchart for Travel to Rental Properties. If you do not have an active rental property business, you add the travel expenses and other investigatory expenses to the cost basis for the property. You then allocate these expenses between the basis for the land and the building.

Example: Ann targets a property for purchase in Miami. She spends $1,000 in travel costs looking at the property and getting a preliminary inspection. If she buys the property, she adds the $1,000 to her cost basis and allocates it between the land and building basis.

 Sandy's elaboration: It is even more important to tie down your initial tax basis for rental investments than it is for your home. This is because the tax basis for rental property is your foundation for taking depreciation deductions. The procedures for establishing the initial tax basis for rental property are similar to those for a home.

If you buy the property and have an active rental property business, you deduct the first $5,000 of travel expenses and amortize any excess over 180 months for expenses incurred after October 22, 2004. If your investigatory expenses exceed $50,000, you may get only a portion of your investigatory expenses. The deduction phases out on expenses of more than $50,000.

This rule came into effect on October 23, 2004 as a result of "tax simplification," which is why it is so complicated. Why can't Congress just give us deductions without some idiotic phase-out rule? All investigatory expenses incurred before this date for active real estate businesses were amortized over 72 months. If you ever want Congress to change the tax code, be careful what you wish for—you may get it.

Summary

- If you incur travel expenses while looking for property, use the travel flowchart on the next page.
- You may deduct travel expenses to look for property if you are traveling in a location where you own rental property and are in an active rental property business (six or more rental units).

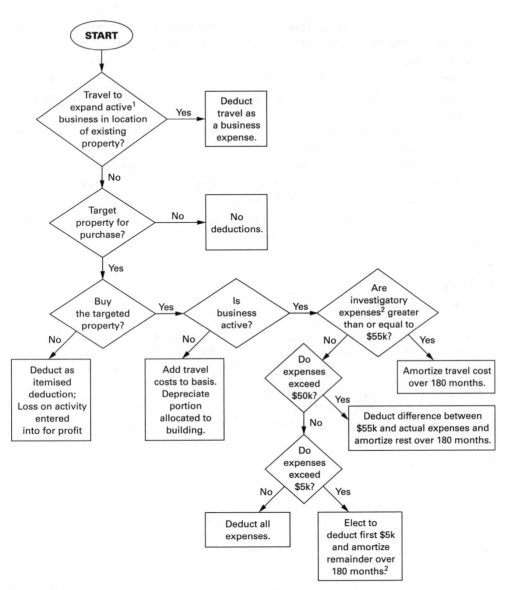

[1] An "active business" requires six or more rental properties.

[2] This applies to all investigatory travel expenses incurred after 10/22/04. See section 195(i)(1) of the IRC.

Note: Travel expenses incurred before 10/23/04 are amortized over 60 months.

Figure 17-1

- If you are not in an active rental property business or didn't look at property in the location of existing property, you must target a specific property to get a deduction.
- If you targeted a specific property but didn't buy it and aren't in an active rental property business, you may deduct the travel expenses as an itemized deduction.
- If you bought the targeted property but aren't in an active rental property business, you add the travel costs to basis.
- If you bought the property and are in an active rental property business, you can deduct the first $5,000 of travel costs and amortize any excess over 180 months. This is an election that must be made on your tax return.
- If your travel and other investigatory expenses exceed $50,000, you will lose some of your investigatory expenses.

Notes

1 Sections 263 and 1012 of the IRC
2 Sections 167 and 168 of the IRC
3 Section 165 of the IRC and Rev. Rul. 77-254, 1977-2 CB 63
4 *Seed vs. Commissioner*, 52 TC 880 (1969), Acq. 1970-2 CB 21; Rev. Rul. 77-254, 1977-2 CB. 63. See also *Mid-State Product Co. vs. Comm.*, 21 TC 696 (1954), Acq. 1955-2 CB 7
5 See footnote 4, *ibid*
6 *Fairey vs. Comm.*, 43 TCM 1169 (1982)
7 *Curphey vs. Comm.*, 73 TC 766 (1980)
8 See footnote 6, *ibid*

Part 5

Tax Goodies Incurred while Owning Rental Property

This part covers ways to minimize the passive loss limits; some nice tax-planning techniques for maximizing depreciation and making land deductible; time-tested, income-splitting techniques that you can use to substantially lower your tax bite and get the equivalent of a deduction for your kid's college education and wedding; and why you should classify fix-up expenses incurred on investment real estate as repairs and not as improvements.

18

Minimizing Passive Loss Problems

Just let 'em feel that you can save 'em something on taxes and nobody will keep you out.

–Warren Buffett

Overview

1. Understand the limitations on real estate losses and the purpose of passive loss rules
2. Learn that passive losses are never lost, just suspended
3. Learn how passive loss rules work
4. Learn why the sale of a property frees suspended losses
5. Learn about the $25,000 loss deduction allowed for real estate investments
6. Understand how being a real estate professional or marrying one can make you rich
7. Understand why you must actively participate in the management of your rental property to fully use the losses

Years ago on the cover of *Newsweek* was a picture of several people toasting each other because they paid no taxes due to real estate and other tax shelter ownership. At the time, rental property losses could shelter any form of income, as could losses derived from limited partnerships. If you owned enough real estate or the right limited partnerships, you didn't pay any income tax.

It became clear to Congress that high marginal rates and the prevalence of tax shelters were causing taxpayers to lose faith in the federal tax system due to a perception that it was unfair and that taxes were paid only by the naive and unsophisticated.[1] Congress then passed the passive loss limitation.

The thrust of passive loss limitation was to prevent you from offsetting losses from passive activities against compensation income and income from portfolio investments (such as interest and dividends).[2] The good news

109

is that Congress left some exceptions that allow people who know what they are doing to be able to use real estate losses against other income.

What Is a Passive Activity?

A passive activity is income or loss generated from real estate investment as well as income or loss derived from a limited partnership where you do not participate in the management.

General Rule

The passive limitation general rule allows you to deduct passive losses from passive income generated in the same year. Passive activity losses are allowed up to passive activity income. The formula is: passive activity losses = passive income generators (passive activity gains) or PALs = PIGs.

Example: Smith earns $150,000 in wages and owns rental property that produces $20,000 in losses. Because rental property is considered a passive activity, Smith may not use the $20,000 loss against his wages unless he meets one of the exceptions to the passive limitation.

Example: Hermione earns $150,000 in wages from her magical duties and has rental property generating a net income of $15,000. If she buys a new property that generates a $20,000 loss, she may use up to $15,000 of this loss against her other passive activity income. The $5,000 excess loss will not be currently deductible against her income unless she meets one of the exceptions to the passive limitation.

Suspension of Passive Losses

If your passive losses for the year exceed your passive income for the year, you do not get a current deduction for any excess losses. *However, these losses aren't lost; they are suspended to be carried forward to future years.* The suspended losses are allocated to the properties that produced them. In future years, here is what happens.[3]

1. Passive losses generated in future years are offset against passive income generated in future years.
2. If there is excess passive income in future years, the suspended losses can offset it. Suspended losses can be used in the future to offset future passive income.
3. Separate calculation and a separate carry forward schedule must be kept for each property.
4. For computing each property's suspended loss, take the loss from the respective property divided by the total losses from all the properties,

then multiply the result by the net passive losses derived from all properties. The formula is: Passive loss on property/Total losses from all properties combined × Net passive losses for all properties. The following example should explain this rule with greater clarity:

Example: Dan has investments in four houses purchased several years ago. This year's income and losses are as follows:

House A: $10,000 profit
House B: $5,000 loss
House C: $25,000 loss
House D: $20,000 loss
Total passive losses for the year: $50,000
Net passive losses for the year: $40,000

The net passive loss is allocated to the properties that produced the loss in the ratio that they contributed to the net loss as follows:

House B $(5/50 × \$40,000) = \$4,000$

House C $(25/50 × \$40,000) = \$20,000$

House D $(20/50 × \$40,000) = \$16,000$

Total passive loss = $40,000

Sandy's elaboration: Each property has its own share of loss carryovers that can be used against passive gains from that property. You need to keep a carryover schedule for each real estate investment you have.

Exceptions to Passive Loss Limitation

Sale of Passive Property

There are several exceptions to the general rule that states passive losses are limited to passive incomes. The first exception occurs when you dispose of your interest in a passive activity (such as selling the property). The suspended loss offsets gain from the sale of that passive activity, and any excess loss is deducted from all other income.[4]

Sandy's elaboration: This is really nice. If you don't have enough passive income to offset the loss, you will get to use the loss from that property when you sell it. This loss not only offsets any gain from that property, but can be used against any form of income that you have, including wages, interest, dividends, etc. Yummy!

Example 1: Using the above example, if you sell House D (which had $16,000 of suspended loss) for a $10,000 profit, you offset the $10,000 profit with the suspended loss. The remaining $6,000 of suspended loss may be deducted from your other income.

Example 2: If you sell House D at a $9,000 loss, you deduct House D's suspended loss of $16,000 against any other form of income. In addition, your $9,000 loss offsets other capital gains, and you can deduct any excess as ordinary loss against any other form of income.[5]

Sandy's tip: I can't emphasize enough how important it is to keep good records of suspended losses for each property. Having a carry forward schedule for suspended losses, kept on a property-by-property basis, is essential. If you are a realtor, you need to communicate this fact to investors. If you are an accountant or financial planner, you need to communicate this to your clients.

$25,000 Loss Deduction for Rental Property

The second exception to the passive loss limitation applies if your adjusted gross income (AGI) is $100,000 or less. Tax law allows you to deduct up to $25,000 of losses from rental property against all other forms of income if you actively participate in the management of the property.[6] Sadly, what Congress gives, they often take away. This $25,000 deduction phases out at 50 cents on the dollar for anything over $100,000 of AGI.[7]

Example: Mary has an adjusted gross income of $130,000 and net rental property losses of $30,000. If she is an active investor and earns less than $100,000 of AGI, she is able to deduct up to $25,000 of her rental property losses against her earned income. Because she has an AGI over $100,000, she is denied part of her $25,000 loss deduction. She may deduct only $10,000 of her losses.

What is active participation? In order to deduct the full $25,000 of losses from rental property, you must be an active participant in your property. You are an active participant if you can show that you or your spouse participates in management decisions such as:

- Selecting tenants
- Setting rental terms
- Reviewing and authorizing expenses

Sandy's tip: Simply signing the lease satisfies the first two requirements. You can satisfy the third by providing in the management agreement that

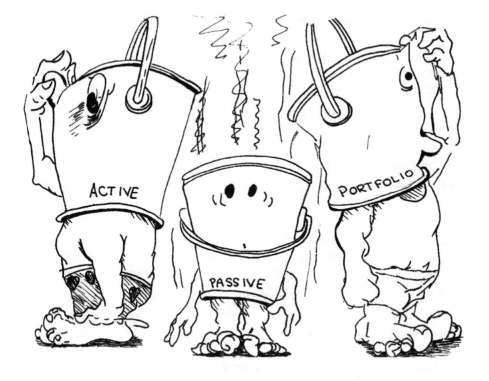

you must review and authorize expenses over a certain limit. You can be an active investor even if you use a management company.

Sandy's elaboration: This $25,000 allowance is designed for middle class Americans. Most middle class American workers don't have a lot of write-offs other than deductions for interest, taxes, and dependents. Being able to take up to $25,000 of real estate losses can be a major help for most middle class workers.

Become or Marry a Real Estate Professional

The third major exception to passive loss limitation allows real estate professionals to write off all passive losses against any income for rental properties in which they materially participate. Thus, rental property is worth more to a real estate professional. Notice, there is no passive loss limitation if either you or your spouse is a real estate professional , and one of you materially participates in the management of the rental properties.

Sandy's elaboration: What is interesting is that you don't have to be a real estate professional yourself. Marrying a real estate professional and materially participating in the management of your properties will qualify for this exception. If your spouse is the qualifying real estate professional, he or she doesn't have to be the one managing the properties. If you are the one who materially participates in the management, your participation is deemed attributable to them.[8]

What Is a Real Estate Professional?

You are a real estate professional when you meet both of the following tests:[9]

1. More than half your work time is in real property trades or businesses in which you materially participate.
2. You spend more than 750 hours working in real property trades or businesses in which you materially participate.

Sandy's elaboration: On a joint return, only one spouse needs to satisfy these requirements.[10]

Real Property Trade or Business

The term "real property trade or business" means any real property development, redevelopment, construction, reconstruction, acquisition, conversion, rental, operation, real estate management, leasing, or brokerage.[11]

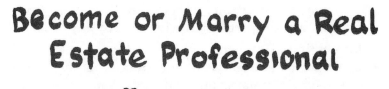

Become or Marry a Real Estate Professional

Sandy's elaboration: This is a fabulous exception for realtors, real estate managers, and developers. If you fall into these categories and manage your properties, you get to write off all real estate losses against your other income with no limitation. WOW!

Material Participation

For the real estate professional exception to apply to the passive loss limitation, you or your spouse must materially participate in the property. You are deemed to materially participate in a property or business if you meet any of the following seven tests:[12]

Test 1: You participate in the activity for more than 500 hours a year.

Example: Monica spends 20 hours a week managing her rental properties. She is deemed to materially participate in this activity.

Test 2: Your participation makes up substantially all of the participation in the activity. Normally, if you are the primary worker, you meet this test. If you or your spouse work in the business or on the rental properties alone, you meet this test. You do not have to meet the 500 hours requirement if you meet Test 2.

Test 3: You participate for more than 100 hours in the activity and that participation is not less than the participation incurred by any other individual.

Example: Bill is employed full-time as an accountant. He also owns interest in a partnership that is engaged in construction activity that is conducted exclusively on Saturdays. Bill and the other partners (Mark and David) are the only participants in the activity. Each Saturday, Bill, Mark, and David work for six hours in the activity. Although Bill does not participate in the activity for more than 500 hours during the taxable year, he is treated as materially participating in the activity because he participates in the activity for more than 100 hours and his participation is not less than the participation of any other individual in the activity for the year.[13]

Sandy's elaboration: This requires only a measly two hours per week managing your properties in order to meet this test.

Test 4: For a trade or business, you participate more than 500 hours in all business ventures and no less than 100 hours in any one business.

Sandy's elaboration: This test doesn't apply to real estate investments unless you are operating a hotel or a bed-and-breakfast type of establishment.

Test 5: You materially participated for 5 of the last 10 years. You use the 500-hour requirement for each year in order to determine material participation during that year.

Example: In 1992, John acquired some rental apartment houses. From 1992 through 1996, he participated in the management of the activity for more than 500 hours. John retired from the activity at the beginning of 1997. He will be deemed as materially participating in the activity for 1997 through 2002 because he materially participated in the activity for 5 years during the 10 years that immediately proceeded each of those years. John will not be treated as materially participating in the activity after 2002 because for those years he did not materially participate in the activity for 5 of the 10 preceding taxable years.[14]

Test 6: The activity is a personal service activity and you materially participate any three years preceding the current year. This test doesn't apply to rental activities. It is designed for those whose main business is accounting, law, health, engineering, architecture, actuarial science, performing arts, consulting, or other businesses that don't have capital as a major factor.

Test 7: Based on all the facts and circumstances, you participate in the activity on a regular, continuous, and substantial basis during the year. For this test to apply, you still need to work on the real estate activities for at least 100 hours per year.[15] Although the regulations don't address when the "facts and circumstances" test is met, the congressional history on this notes that you generally meet this test when:[16] real estate activity is your principal business; you are regularly present at the location of your property; you have a lot of knowledge and experience in the management of rental properties; you make the significant management decisions rather than merely approve decisions by your rental manager.

Sandy's elaboration: In order to be deemed to materially participate in your rental property, you need to meet *any* one of Tests 1, 2, 3, 5, or 7. If you own a hotel or bed-and-breakfast, you need to meet only one of these tests.

Corporate Exception to Passive Loss Limits

Generally, C Corporations are not subject to the passive activity limits.[17] Congress does not want taxpayers to circumvent the rules with a mere change of form in the way that they conduct business, especially if it offsets portfolio income such as interest and dividends.[18] Certain closely held corporations can still avoid the passive loss rules to a limited extent.

What Is a Closely Held C Corporation?

A closely held C Corporation is one whose main business is accounting, law, health, engineering, architecture, actuarial science, performing arts, consulting, or other businesses that don't have capital as a major factor and has five or fewer stockholders owning more than 50% of the value of the stock.[19]

Closely Held C Corporations Can Use Real Estate Losses

A closely held C Corporation is permitted to use passive losses and credits against its net active income, which is its taxable income computed without regard to its portfolio income such as interest and dividends.

Sandy's elaboration: If you are a closely held C Corporation, you can shelter your business income other than what you get from interest, dividends, and stock gains. In addition, gain from certain oil and gas activities conducted by closely held corporations may not be sheltered by real estate losses.

Corporations that are not closely held corporations can use real estate losses to shelter all of their income.

Example: Sheri and her husband own a C Corporation that sells medical supplies. The corporation has taxable income of $200,000, not counting interest and dividends of $20,000. If the corporation owns investment real estate, they may use the losses against their $200,000 of active business income without being subject to the passive loss limits.

Conclusion

Whew! This was a long chapter full of a lot of details. Understanding passive loss limitation rules enables you to take advantage of real estate losses.

Summary

- Passive loss rules were designed to limit the use of real estate and partnership losses against other income. However, there are some exceptions to these rules.
- The general rule for passive losses is that passive activity losses are limited to passive income generators (passive gains).
- Real estate and limited partnerships are considered passive activities.
- Passive losses that aren't currently deductible due to these rules get suspended forever. You can carry them over to future years and offset future passive activity gains.

    There are some exceptions to the passive activity loss limits:
    1. Disposal of the property: If you dispose of a passive activity, you can immediately deduct all suspended losses allocable to that activity or property.
    2. $25,000 loss deduction for active investors of rental property: This applies to those with Adjusted Gross Income of $100,000 or less and who are active investors (investors who approve leases, approve tenants, and approve expenditures). You do not have to manage the properties yourself.
    3. Real estate professional exception: If you or your spouse is a real estate professional and one of you materially participates in the management of your properties, you can use all real estate losses without being subject to the passive loss limits.
    4. Closely held corporation exception: If you are a closely held C Corporation, you may use your corporate-owned real estate against any active taxable income of the corporation. This does not apply to portfolio income such as interest, dividends, and normal stock gains.

Notes

1 S. Rep. 313, 99th Cong., 2d Sess. 713 (1986); H.R. Rep. 426, 99th Cong., 1st Sess. 54 (1985)
2 Section 469 of the IRC
3 Section 469(d)(1) of the IRC
4 Section 469(g) of the IRC
5 Sections 1211 (b)(1) and 1231 of the IRC
6 Section 469(i) of the IRC
7 Section 469(i)(3)(A) of the IRC
8 Section 469(h)(5) of the IRC and 1.469-5T(f)(3) of the Regs
9 469©(7) of the IRC

10 Section 469©(7) of the IRC
11 Section 469©(7)(C) of the IRC
12 Section 1.469-5T(a) of the Regs
13 The example came from Kleinrock, *Analysis and Explanation for Material Participation,* Section 50.8 (2005).
14 *Ibid*
15 Section 1.469-5T(b)(2) of the Regs
16 S. Rep. 313, 99th Cong., 2d Sess. 733-735 (1986)
17 Section 1.469-1T(g) of the Regs
18 S. Rep. 313, 99th Cong., 2d Sess. 713, 722 (1986)
19 Sections 469(j)(1) and 465(a) and 542(a) of the IRC

19

Maximizing Your Depreciation Deductions

Overview

1. Learn about the general rule of land being nondeductible
2. Understand why using an appraiser will get you much better results than using the county land assessor's appraisal
3. Understand the basis rules for clearing, grading, and landscaping
4. Learn about the 20-foot rule for landscaping

A government that robs Peter to pay Paul can always depend on the support of Paul.
—George Bernard Shaw

When you purchase investment property, tax law requires you to allocate your purchase price between land, buildings, and equipment and to have support for this allocation.[1] The reason is that buildings and equipment are depreciable and land is not.[2] You must allocate the tax basis of rental property between the land and the building. As an asset that gives you tax benefits, land is useless.

Hot tip: You should do everything in your power to make the cost allocated to land as small as possible and to the building and equipment as large as possible. If your goal is to improve profits, make land less valuable.

Two Sources of Allocation

The worst allocation source is the assessor's property tax values. Unfortunately, many property tax assessors are not careful with the split between land and building. In many cases, they allocate heavily toward the land. Yuck! This is because if the building is destroyed, there will be less hassle with a new property assessment. After all, land is forever. Using an assessor's allocation tends to result in the lowest depreciation deductions because they usually allocate too much to the land. If you do use the property tax bill as your basis for the allocation, you simply apply the relationship from the bill to your property.

Example: Richard's assessment to the land is $60,000 and improvements are $140,000. The total assessment to the property is $200,000. If Mary buys Richard's property for $300,000 and uses the assessment, she will allocate $90,000 to the land and $210,000 to the improvements.

Because tax assessors tend to be inflexible and usually have a detrimental allocation to the land, you may want to spend money getting an independent appraisal. When you meet with an appraiser, tell her your goals and ask if she can meet them (which means giving you a better allocation than that provided by the assessor). She will tell you if she can be of service and will be able to explain what tools she uses. In addition, she can explain her fees. All this can be accomplished in your first meeting. This way, you will know if it is worthwhile to spend the money on an independent appraisal.

Sandy's elaboration: If you fail to use your own appraiser, the IRS usually requires taxpayers to allocate their basis between land and other improvements based on the assessed value.[3]

Appraisers have a variety of tools and techniques at their disposal, including an income analysis technique that values assets based on earnings potential over the life of rental or business assets. If you plan to improve the property, the appraiser may use the building residual technique to push more cost to the building. Because the appraisal must stand up to IRS scrutiny, make sure you use a qualified appraiser.

Bottom Line

Remember, from a tax-benefit view, buildings are beautiful and land is ugly. Pay attention to your land and building allocations because, once made, you keep them for the entire time that you keep the property.

If you use an independent appraiser, put a copy of the appraisal in your permanent file next to the property purchase documents.

Clearing and Grading Costs

The costs of general-purpose clearing and grading necessary to adapt land to specific use are part of the cost of land.[4] Your tax plan should include keeping your clearing and grading costs to a minimum.

Depreciate Landscaping and Shrubbery Near the Building

The cost of landscaping and shrubbery are depreciable when it is in the right location. Landscaping and shrubs generally located within 20 feet of the building or other structures are depreciable when destruction of the building also destroys the shrubs and landscaping.[5] Thus, any landscaping or shrubs that you will not destroy when you destroy the building are considered land.

Getting Land Ready for a Building

The cost of digging a hole and removing the soil to set the building becomes a cost of the depreciable building rather than a cost that is allocated to the land.[6] Demolition costs, which are incurred right after you acquire the property, are added to the basis of the land.[7]

Sandy's elaboration: The regulations provide an exception if demolition did not take place immediately and the building was being rented or used in a trade or business. In that case, the owner is permitted to allocate a portion of the basis to the building and recover this basis over the period the building was rented or used in a trade or business.[8]

Example: Howard purchased an old house for $100,000, which he intended to demolish in order to build a new office for his accounting practice. His lease in the building where his practice was located would not expire for

another three years. Therefore, Howard rented the house to students at the local university until just before his lease expired. As soon as the residential lease expired, Howard demolished the house at a cost of $10,000. At the time of the purchase, Howard may allocate a portion of the $70,000 cost to the house equal to the present value of the future rent payments and depreciate that amount over three years. The remaining cost, as well as the $10,000 cost of demolition, is allocated to the basis in the land.[9]

Sandy's tip: If you want to increase your depreciation deductions, do not demolish. Consider remodeling and expanding instead.

Summary

- Land isn't depreciable. Buildings and equipment are depreciable.
- When you buy investment property, allocate as much as possible to the building and equipment and as little as possible to the land.
- Use your own appraiser to maximize the allocation to the land and equipment and to minimize the allocation to the land.
- If you don't use your own appraiser soon after acquiring the investment property, you will need to use the assessor's allocation. Either way, for investment property, some allocation must be made.
- As a general rule, clearing and grading costs are allocated to the land.

- Clearing and grading costs within 20 feet of the building, as well as landscaping that would be destroyed if the building were demolished, is allocated to the basis of the building.
- Costs incurred for digging a hole and removing soil in order to set a building are allocated to the basis of the building.
- Demolition costs incurred soon after property acquisition are allocated to the basis of the land unless they occur at least one year after acquiring a property that is rented out before demolition.
- Generally, don't demolish—remodel and expand.

Notes

1 *Tunnell vs. U.S.*, 512 F.2d 1192 (3rd Cir.), cert denied. *Aurora Village Shopping Center vs. Comm.*, 29 TCM 126 (1970). See also section 1.167(a)-5 of the Regs
2 Section 1.167(a)-2, 1.167(a)-5 and Proposed Reg 1.168-3(a)(1) of the Regs
3 *Meiers vs. Comm.*, T.C. Memo 1982-51
4 Rev. Rul. 65-265,1965-2 C.B.52 as clarified by Rev. Rul. 68-193, 1968-1 C.B. 79
5 See footnote 4, *ibid*. See also Rev. Rul. 74-265, 1974-1 C.B. 56
6 Rev. Rul. 65-265, 1965-2 C.B. 52
7 Section 280B and 280B(2) of the IRC
8 Section 1.165-3(a)(2) of the Regs
9 Kleinrock's Analysis and Explanation, Section 66,9 (2005)

20

Making Land Deductible

If the IRS took 100 taxpayers at random and sent each an incorrect notice that they owed an extra $92.35 in taxes and interest, more than two-thirds would probably just send in a check without investigating further.

—G. Guttman

Overview

1. Learn the techniques of how the rich make land deductible
2. Understand how to deduct equipment twice
3. Learn about the technique of sale-leaseback
4. Understand the financial planning technique known as gift-leaseback
5. Learn about the strategy known as the gift to push tax technique

The concept of income splitting is not new. Financial and tax planners have been using these techniques in varying forms for many years with rich clients. This chapter and the next inform you of what wealthy taxpayers have been doing to significantly reduce their taxes.

Income Splitting

The concept behind income splitting is simple: several taxpayers with lower tax brackets pay less tax on the same income as that of one taxpayer with a high tax bracket.

Example: Sam and Jean have $100,000 of rental income (plus other earned income) that is taxed at:

- 35 percent federal rate

- 8 percent state rate

If they transfer the property to their five children, each child pays tax on one-fifth of the rent at their individual tax bracket. The family saves $22,150:

127

Tax on $100,000 at parents' bracket: $43,000
Tax on $20,000 at children's tax bracket: $4,170
Number of children: ×5
Total federal and state tax for children: $20,850
Annual savings: $22,150

 Sandy's elaboration: If you have children who plan to attend college, you can pay for their schooling using after-tax money. If you split income, you give them untaxed money. They pay tax in their lower tax bracket and use the larger after-tax balance for school. Pretty nifty!

Type of Income to Split

If you own rental property, you may have the perfect opportunity to split income. Land is not depreciable, so it produces no tax shelter. Rent on the land or equipment used in business is deductible.[1] If your children own the land and rent it to you, they receive taxable income at low tax rates and you get a deduction at your high tax bracket.

Technique 1: Buy the Land Separately

The best time to split the land from the building is at purchase. In 2006, you and your spouse could give $24,000 each to as many people as you wanted without a gift tax. For both 2005 and 2006, you get a lifetime exemption of $1,000,000 in addition to the yearly exemptions. Therefore, you can give away a lot of property.

Sandy's elaboration: You accomplish this by having your children own the land where the building is located. They have title to the land, which is in trust, and you own the building. You rent the land from them in the form of ground rent. This allows you to depreciate the building and deduct the rent that you are paying to your children's trust for the land. In this way, you deduct 100 percent of the land! Isn't this neat?

If you own investment property, get an appraisal of the land, transfer the title to a trust, then rent the land from the trust.

Caution: Of all the techniques, this one especially must be undertaken carefully, using the services of a real estate and/or tax attorney. The ground rent must be reasonable.

Technique 2: Give the Property to Relatives Age 18 or Over

With this strategy, you give appreciated property to a relative who is at least age 18. The lower-bracket relative sells the property and pays the tax.

Result: Both you and your recipient have more cash to spend because Uncle Sam took less from the person in the lower tax bracket.

Rationale: President Bush and Congress made a huge mistake by creating a tax loophole. If you sell capital gains property that you have held for over a year, you pay federal income tax of 25 percent on depreciation and a maximum of 15 percent on appreciation,[2] in addition to state taxes.

If you are, however, in the 10 to 15 percent federal tax bracket, the maximum federal long-term capital gains rate is only 5 percent.

Example: Colin owns investment real estate that has appreciated $100,000 over the original cost. If he takes $10,000 in depreciation, he pays tax at a rate of 25 percent on depreciation and 15 percent on $100,000 of appreciation, making his total federal tax $17,500. If he transfers the property to his children, who are in the 10 percent tax bracket, their federal long-term capital gains rate drops to 5 percent on the appreciation. They pay tax at their ordinary tax rate (assumed to be 10 percent) on the depreciation. They pay $6,000 in tax on the same property—a savings of $11,500.

Sandy's elaboration: The wealthy have been using this technique for years by simply giving away appreciated real estate or stock to their lower-bracket children or grandchildren and letting them sell the property. Title transfer to the recipients must be made before you have a contract for sale.

This works with anyone who passes the "mirror test." What is the "mirror test?" Take a mirror and put it inside a freezer overnight. The next morning, take the mirror out and place it under the nose of a person who is in a lower tax bracket than you. If they can fog the mirror, you can use this technique with them.

Therefore, this technique will work for any lower-tax-bracket folks whom you would support, such as your parents, nieces, nephews, significant other, etc.

Gift tax rule for singles: In 2006, you can give away $12,000 to as many people as you want without having to worry about tax rules.[3] The gift tax exemption for 2005 was $11,000 per person.

You don't get a tax deduction for the gift, but the recipient doesn't pay tax on it.[4] It is a free move of your money or assets as far as income tax is concerned. This amount gets indexed for inflation and will go up about every two years.

Gift rule for married people: In 2006, married people could give away up to $24,000 ($22,000 in 2005) to any number of persons without incurring a gift tax.[5] Single people can give away $12,000 worth of property to each recipient, gift tax free. When a gift to an individual exceeds the $12,000 threshold, both spouses must agree it is a joint gift, and a gift tax return must be filed.[6] For gifts of $12,000 or less in 2006 ($11,000 or less in 2005), no gift tax return need be filed.[7] There is a $1,000,000 lifetime gift tax exemption in addition to the yearly exclusions.

 Sandy's elaboration: When I say you can give away $12,000 if single, or $24,000 if married, this amount is based on fair market value of the item given away at the date the property is transferred.[8] The basis for computing gain and holding period of the property given away is the basis and holding period of the donor.[9]

Example: John gives his children some stock that cost him $20 per share and had a fair market value as of the date of the gift of $60. If John has held the stock for two years, his children's basis and holding period is John's basis and holding period ($20 and two years).

 Sandy's elaboration: If you give away property with a basis that is more than fair market value as of the date of the gift, the recipient's basis for gain is your basis; however, if the recipient sells the property for a loss, their basis is the lower fair market value as of the date of the gift. Thus, do not give away property that has a fair market value of less than your basis. If it is investment or business property, sell it and take the loss.

 Kiddie Tax problem: The gift to push tax technique is such a good technique and so widely used among the rich that Congress tried to curtail the use of it by implementing what accountants call the Kiddie Tax.

Children under age 18 paid tax on investment income in excess of $1,700 in 2006 ($1,600 in 2005) at the highest earning parent's tax rate.[10]

If your children are at least 18 years old by December 31, the Kiddie Tax does not apply—they are taxed on investment earnings at their own tax brackets.

Example: Jim and Sue's son, Alan, is 12 years old in 2006 and earns $2,000 of interest. Under the Kiddie Tax, Alan reports $1,700 on his tax return and pays tax at his normal tax rate. The other $300 is taxed at the higher tax bracket of Jim or Sue.

Sandy's elaboration: The gift to push tax technique and renting land from your children works if the children are at least age 18 by December 31. It will also work even if they are under age 18, if the total is less than $1,700 (in 2006) for each child.

Technique 3: The Botkin Gift-Leaseback Technique

How would you like to deduct equipment used in real estate twice? No, this is not a typographical error. This technique involves depreciating equipment used on investment property (washers, dryers, refrigerators, dishwashers, furniture, etc.) and giving title to the property to your lower-tax-bracket relatives. You then lease the equipment back, paying monthly rent. In this way, you depreciated the equipment and are now deducting the lease payments to your relatives. The result is that you deduct equipment used on your rental property twice!

Sandy's elaboration: All equipment in real estate gets depreciated separately from the rental property.

Example: Murray rents the equipment used in his rental properties from his son's trust. His son charges him $2,600 per year in rent. Assuming that Murray is in the 45 percent federal and state bracket, his taxes are now reduced by $1,170. His 18-year-old son, who is in college, receives $2,600 from the trust and pays tax of $196. The family unit receives a net tax benefit of $974 from equipment that otherwise would have produced no tax benefit because the equipment was previously depreciated.

You need to give the right property: To put the gift-leaseback strategy to work, you must own the asset. As an individual, you may gift assets to anyone.[11] Your regular, C corporation may not, however, make such gifts.[12]

Fully depreciated property produces the maximum deductions for the gift-leaseback strategy because you have already depreciated the assets. Fully depreciated assets produce no tax deductions. However, by using fully depreciated assets, you are creating new deductions because the Botkin gift-leaseback technique creates a new rental deduction.

The key is that you give away property that you are using in your business or investment property but may not want years from now.

Minors: If you make a gift to a minor, you may have to use an irrevocable trust to make it proper. It is important that an independent trustee be used for all trusts and that the trust corpus and income not be returned to you.[13]

Caution: Don't give the recipient the ability to return the property to you because if the property is returned to you, you will be taxed on the income from the trust.

Sandy's elaboration: Another big advantage of the gift-leaseback technique is asset protection. People are spending thousands to learn about asset protection. You can simply and cheaply transfer property into trust for your family and lease it from them. If you are sued after this transaction has occurred, those assets will be protected from creditors because you are no longer the owner.

Technique 4: Sell Assets to Lower-Bracket Friends or Relatives Age 18 or Over and Lease Back

This is very similar to Technique 3, so everything said there also applies here. It varies in that you are selling property that you have either already depreciated or are not getting any tax benefits from, then leasing the property back. In essence, you are putting a friend or relative in the leasing business, but it allows you to select the assets used.

Example: Maynard has no mortgage left on his $500,000 home that he bought for $250,000. Because he has no mortgage, he gets little write-offs for his home. It being a principal residence, he can't deduct repairs on the home either. Using the sale-leaseback, Maynard sells the house to his two sons at fair market value, taking an installment note of $496,000 at 5 percent. He rents the house back from his sons at fair market rent. In essence Maynard is financing his sons' purchase of the house.

Result: Maynard won't pay any income tax because his gain is less than or equal to the exclusionary amount, which is $250,000. Maynard and his sons have an almost equal cash flow because they are receiving rent to help offset the note payments. In addition, only the note will be in Maynard's estate. All appreciation in the real estate will accrue to his sons outside of the estate. If the property needs repairs, his sons may deduct the repairs because it is investment property. Further, Maynard's sons now each deduct their share of the property because they are landlords. Finally, his sons may visit Maynard once a year as a tax-deductible caretaking trip.

Consider a private annuity: Instead of financing the purchase with a note, the sons can pay a setup for the life of Maynard. This is called a private annuity. The advantages of a private annuity are that no note is included in the estate upon Maynard's death and there are no estate taxes or income tax recapture problems.

Sandy's elaboration: The techniques noted in this chapter must be done correctly;[14] the lease should be for a short term and can be renewable from year to year. It definitely should not have a term that exceeds the seller's life expectancy. The rent and the sale price should be at fair market value. All payments should be made to the appropriate parties. No forgiveness of any payment should occur. Get a lawyer to structure a sale-leaseback or gift-leaseback.

In addition, you should have a valid business purpose for each step in the transaction.[15] The person who buys your home should acquire and retain significant and genuine attributes of a traditional owner, including the benefits and burdens of ownership.

Document nontax business reason: Many courts[16] require a nontax reason for a sale-leaseback or gift-leaseback. A letter from a lawyer stating that this transaction is recommended for any of the following should be enough:

- Protection from creditors
- Avoidance of ethical conflicts
- Provisions for professional management
- Avoidance of problems with shareholders and/or business associates
- Avoidance of estate tax or probate

Caution: If you want to use sale-leaseback of your home to your relatives, do so only if the recognized gain will be less than the universal exclusion—otherwise you may have to pay tax at ordinary income rates without receiving the cash. The recipient must also keep the property for at least two years or gain from the installment note will be triggered.

Summary

- Splitting income among family members can save a bundle in taxes.
- Put the title to the land that underlies rental property in trust for your relatives and lease it back from the trust.
- Use the gift to push tax technique to transfer real estate to your lower-tax-bracket relatives and let them sell it. This could eliminate as much as 66 percent of the capital gains tax.
- Be careful of the Kiddie Tax if your children are under age 18 on December 31.
- Use the gift-leaseback technique to deduct equipment twice. In addition, use the technique to deduct the equivalent of the land.
- Consider the sale-leaseback technique for your principal residence as long as the exclusion exceeds the gain.

Notes

1 Sections 162(a)(3) and 212 of the IRC
2 Sections 1(h) of the IRC. See also Notice 97-59, 1997-2 C.B. 309.
3 Section 2503(b) of the IRC
4 Sections 274(b)(1) and 102(a) of the IRC
5 Section 2513(a) of the IRC and 25.2513-1(c) of the Regs
6 Sections 6019 and 2503(b) of the IRC
7 *Ibid*
8 Section 2512(a) of the IRC and 25-2513-1(c) of the Regs
9 Sections 1015(a) and 1223(2) of the IRC
10 Sections 1(i) and 1(g) of the IRC. See also Rev. Proc. 2003-85, 2003-2 C.B. 1184 and Rev. Proc. 2005-70, 2005-47 I.R.B.
11 Section 2503(b) of the IRC
12 *E.g. Epstein vs. Commissioner*, 53 T.C. 459 (1969), Acq. 1970-2 C.B. 19
13 Section 673(a) of the IRC
14 *Estate of Maxwell*, 98 T.C. 39 (1992)
15 IRS Notice 2005-13
16 *Matthews vs. Commissioner*, 61 T.C. 12 (1973), rev'd 75-2 U.S.T.C. Par 967 (5th Cir. 1975). See also *Frank Lyons Co. vs. Comm.*, 435 U.S. 561 (S. Ct. 1978)

21

Splitting Income by Hiring Family Members

A fool and his money are soon parted. It takes creative tax laws for the rest.
—Bob Thaves

Overview

1. Learn how hiring family members can reduce your taxes by thousands
2. Understand how some children can be exempt from Social Security and federal income tax
3. Learn what documentation is needed in order to bulletproof hiring relatives from even the toughest IRS agent

Hiring Spouses to Work on Your Rental Property

Wages paid by husband to wife or by wife to husband are subject to Social Security tax.[1] There is no benefit in trying to qualify for extra social security retirement monies by paying extra social security taxes; accordingly, pay your spouse as little as possible and give him or her tax-free fringe benefits—as discussed in my book, *Lower Your Taxes—BIG TIME*, which is available at Barnes and Noble, Amazon.com, Border's Books, and my Web site (www.taxreductioninstitute.com). Some examples of fringe benefits are paying for health insurance and setting up a self-insured medical plan that pays for all medical expenses that aren't covered by insurance. A self- insured medical plan can cover expenses that are not covered by your medical insurance such as the deductibles, coinsurance, braces, dental, mileage to the doctor and dentist, routine physicals, etc.

Employment of your spouse must be bona fide[2] for the work that they undertake on your rental property. The IRS will, as it should, question whether your spouse did any work. You must have evidence of actual work done for this deduction to withstand IRS scrutiny.

135

Employing Children to Work on Your Rental Property

I am often asked if the cost of college tuition, room and board, cars for children, and weddings are deductible. Regretfully, I tell people that these items are not deductible. However, as I am fond of saying, "Where there is a will.....there's a lawyer." How would you like to get the equivalent of a deduction for all these items? The way to do that is to hire your children to work in your rental property business.

Reasonable wages paid to work on rental property are deductible on Schedule E of your tax return, unless you have a hotel or a bed-and-breakfast, in which case those wages are deductible on Schedule C. If you pay your children deducible wages and they use that money to pay for their own tuition, cars, room and board, and books, aren't you getting the equivalent of a deduction for all these items?

Perspective

In effect, Uncle Sam underwrites the education, weddings, and other uses for your children's money.

Sandy's elaboration: What kind of work can children perform on rental property? Among other things, they can mow lawns, paint houses, make repairs, work on your computer, or shred documents.

In 2006, the first $5,150 was tax-free because they got a standard deduction against any wages of $5,150.[3] In 2005, this standard deduction was $5,000. Therefore, in 2006 the first $5,150 they earn in wages is tax-free. In addition, the first $7,300 above the standard deduction is taxed at the 10 percent bracket. If you are in the 35 percent federal tax bracket, the $5,150 produces a tax savings of $1,802 from federal taxes plus a potential savings of $149 from the Medicare surcharge.

Example: You pay your daughter $5,150 to work on your rental property. You deduct it as reasonable wages. She is under age 18 and you are not incorporated, so you pay no social security or unemployment taxes. Your daughter reports the $5,150 on her tax return and she claims a standard deduction of $5,150 (in 2006) against wages. The result is that the money she receives is tax-free!

Another question I get a lot in my seminars is "How old must my children be in order to hire them?" The answer is age seven or older. The age seven or older rule comes from the Eller case[4] in which Eller hired his three children, including the youngest, who was age seven. The IRS contested the employment of the seven-year-old but lost in court.

Caution: For wages to family members to be deductible, they must perform some work on the properties. I have a friend who did just what Eller did. He hired his children to work as janitors in his manufacturing plant during the summers. All wages were paid by check. He kept time sheets for the work performed and the wages were reasonable. The auditing IRS agent asked one of the kids where the bathroom was, but the kid (janitor) didn't know. The agent then disallowed all deductions for wages from these family members. If you are going to hire your children or spouse, always show them where the bathrooms are located. If they don't legitimately work in your business or rental properties, you can't pay them a deductible wage. It's that simple.

Setting Your Child's Salary

Unlike that of your spouse, you want to pay your child as much as possible because there is no payroll tax penalty on the wages, assuming they are under age 18 and you are not incorporated. The salary or wage you pay must be reasonable in order to be deductible.[5] This means that the amount you pay for services must be similar to amounts paid for similar services by similar businesses under similar circumstances.[6] When setting the salary, be sure to allow for the experience or inexperience and ability

Split the Income

of your child. Also, consider the 10 factors that the IRS uses to examine wages for reasonableness:[7]

- Duties performed
- Volume of work
- Type and amount of responsibility
- Complexity of work
- Amount of time required for the work
- Cost of living in the area
- Ability and achievements of the employee
- Comparison of amount of salary to business income
- Your pay policy regarding all employees (if there are other employees)
- Income history of the employee

Sandy's elaboration: It is essential that you pay your kids a reasonable wage for what they do. For example, paying a child $40,000 for filing three hours a week isn't reasonable. Meet with your accountant about setting up a reasonable wage for the hours and duties worked by all relatives. You can also go to www.salary.com and find comparable salaries for similar work and use their data as a basis for setting a reasonable hourly wage.

Documentation Strategies for Employing Relatives

If you were an IRS auditor, would you really believe that someone's spouse or child was a bona fide employee? You would only if you saw adequate proof. In most cases, it's absolutely essential that your relatives fill out either a tax diary or timesheets at the end of each week. To get your deductions for wages, you must be able to prove what work was actually performed.[8] Each day your relative works, the time sheet or tax organizer should show:

- Date
- Description of tasks performed
- Hours worked

Documentation Tip

At the end of each day or week, you should approve the time sheet for payment. Payment to your spouse or child should always be made by check. Even if your child is too young to have a checking account, you should pay by check and deposit the funds in your kid's name. In this circumstance, establish a custodial account at your local bank. The check completes the audit trail by establishing that you paid the child or spouse and that the child or spouse actually received the payment.

Get an Employment Contract

Have your lawyer draft an employment contract noting pay rate, duties, benefits, etc. Pay should be based on the hours worked.[9] As an alternative, you can go to an office supply house and get an employment contract. You need your child's social security number to complete the payroll paperwork. The social security number should be obtained when the child in born.

Sandy's elaboration: When you hire someone, you might want to use a payroll service for all the paperwork. They will do all the filings and either issue a check to your employee or directly deposit the funds in his or her account. There are a number of good payroll services such as ADP, Paychecks, Tax Sentinel I, etc.

Summary

- Hire your spouse to work on your rental property and pay him or her minimum wage. Pay for as much tax-free fringe benefits as legally possible.
- Hire your children to work on your rental property. Reasonable wages for bona fide work are fully deductible, and the first $5,150 of wages in 2006 is tax-free.
- Don't forget that wages paid to your children under age 18 from an unincorporated business are exempt from social security and federal unemployment tax.
- All family members should fill out time sheets, a tax diary, or tax organizer showing what they did from week to week and the hours worked.
- Use a payroll service for the filling of all IRS and state paperwork.
- For more information on fringe benefits and hiring relatives, go to my Web site at www.taxreductioninstitute.com to obtain *Tax Strategies for Business Professionals* and my book, *Lower Your Taxes—BIG TIME*.

Notes

1 Sections 3121(b)(3)(A) and 3306(c)(5) of the IRC
2 Section 1.162-7(a) of the Regs
3 Section 63(h)(2) of the IRC
4 *Eller vs. Comm.*, 77 T.C. 934; *Acq.* 1984-2 C.B. 1
5 Section 162(a)(1) of the IRC. In addition, the expenses must be ordinary and necessary for your business to be deductible. This also applies to hiring any relative or friend.
6 Section 1.162-7(b)(3) of the Regs
7 IRS Publication 535 (2004)
8 Section 1.162-7(a) of the Regs
9 *Haeder vs. Comm.*, T.C. Memo 2000-7

22

Why Repairs on Investment Property Are Important

The best things in life are free, but sooner or later the government will find a way to tax them.

—Anonymous

Overview
1. Learn why repairing investment property is worth more than making improvements on the same property
2. Understand the distinction courts use to determine what constitutes repairs and what constitutes improvements
3. Learn how to build a case for repairs using six time-tested strategies

Those who don't apply the information in this chapter could lose thousands on each investment property each year. Read this chapter very carefully and fully understand what is contained herein.

The key behind repairs is that you want all fix-ups to your rental property to be classified as repairs, not improvements. Say that several times so this point will stay with you forever. Repairs are deductible when incurred. Improvements are capital expenditures that you write off over 27.5 years for residential rental property[1] (39 years for commercial property).[2]

Example: Marc spends $10,000 on a fix-up. If he classifies it correctly as a repair, he gets an immediate deduction of $10,000. If, however, he classifies it as an improvement on his residential rental property, he deducts the $10,000 over 27.5 years, resulting in a yearly deduction of $364. In today's dollars that would be worth about $4,840.

Sandy's elaboration: Putting it another way, a repair is about twice as valuable as an improvement.

Fix-up for Homes and Principal Residences

Remember what we discussed in Chapter 5, which deals with home improvements? We noted that for principal residences and for second homes, you want your fix-up to be properly classified as an improvement, not a repair. Thus, with your home, the result is just the opposite of what you want for rental property because home repairs are nondeductible personal expenditures for principal residences, which give you no tax benefits. Home improvements, on the other hand, are capital expenditures and add to the home's tax basis.

For residential rentals and commercial property, you want repairs because they are immediately deductible.

What Is a Repair?

A repair mends or restores to a sound state. You make a repair to keep the property in ordinary, efficient operating condition. It does not add to the value of the property, nor does it appreciably prolong its life.[3] It merely keeps the property useable and operating over its probable life.[4]

Improvements

Improvements are depreciated, which take many years to deduct. You make improvements to:[5]

- Increase the value of the property
- Make the property last longer
- Adapt the property to a new and different use

Gray Area

The difference between a repair and an improvement rests on the facts and circumstances of each case. As you may suspect, there is considerable disagreement over the definitions.[6] An improvement or a repair is a matter of fact. Get a feel for how the courts and the IRS view these facts, then you can plan accordingly.

If you spend money to make property last longer or to increase its market value, you have made an improvement.[7] If the purpose for which money was spent does not add greatly to the life or increase the current value of the property, it is a repair.[8] You can tell from the definition that there is considerable gray area where the facts are subject to wide interpretation. However, if you know what you are doing, you can be quite aggressive with the IRS and usually win.

Example: When does work on a roof cease to be a repair and become a partial replacement? In situations of this sort, knowledge, along with good tax planning and having complete records, can yield big tax savings.

The Jacobson Case[9]

This was the first major case that really illustrated what you need to do. Roger Jacobson bought a four-unit apartment for $30,000 (obviously this happened many years ago). It had one tenant and the building was in poor shape. Jacobson spent $6,247 with a contractor to:

- Remove tree limbs that were rubbing on the roof
- Repair water damage
- Repair electrical wiring
- Clean the carpet, floors, and building exterior
- Repair the front porch
- Install new cabinet doors
- Install new Formica tops

The IRS said that all the work was an improvement. Jacobson took the matter to court. The tax court allowed $5,000 of the $6,247 as a deductible repair and made Jacobson capitalize the remaining $1,247 for the new cabinet doors and Formica tops. In siding with Jacobson, the court noted that:

- There was a tenant in residence.
- The presence of a tenant meant that the property was commercially active.
- The $6,247 total and the $5,000 allowed as a repair were not material based on a $30,000 price.

Sandy's elaboration: If the improvements had cost more than the repairs, Jacobson might have been in trouble. Keep improvements at less than repairs, and keep improvements at less than 25 percent of the purchase price. The word "new" signals improvements rather than replacement or repair.[10] A combination of good planning and good records of proof are crucial to repair deductions. There are many fix-ups you can classify in either category.

Building a Case for Repairs

Is it a repair? Is it an improvement? Remember, most money spent to fix up property does not fall at polar ends of the repair or improvement scale.

Two taxpayers can spend the same money doing the same fix-up and obtain totally different results. It is a question of facts and how you present and establish them.

Six Strategies to Bulletproof Repairs

From reading many of the leading cases on the subject, there are six strategies you can follow to help ensure your fix-ups are good-looking repairs, not ugly improvements on rental property:

1. Segregate repairs from improvements
2. Fix minor portions only
3. Use similar, comparable, or less expensive materials
4. Fix damages only
5. Repair after an event
6. Repair during occupancy or between tenants

Let's examine each of these strategies in detail.

Strategy 1–Segregate repairs from improvements: If you are going to renovate the property and make repairs, you must segregate repairs from improvements in order to deduct the repairs.[11] The IRS, in its audit manual, says that fix-ups that would be a repair when made separately are improvements when made as part of a general overhaul of the building.[12] Make sure repairs are not part of an overall plan. If possible, have repairs done by separate contractors.

Strategy 2–Fix a minor portion only: If you are replacing an entire wall, roof, or floor, you are usually making an improvement.[13] If your purpose is to have an improvement, use better-quality materials than what were used originally or use improvement materials.[14]

Example: Fixing part of a shingled roof with slate is an improvement. Fixing a part of a shingled roof with shingles is a repair.

Strategy 3–Use similar, comparable, or less expensive materials: If your purpose is to mend or restore to a sound state, use comparable materials.[15] If your purpose is to improve, use better quality or improved materials.[16]

Strategy 4–Fix damages only: If you want to classify your fix-ups as repairs, replace or restore worn out, broken, and deteriorated parts of the property.[17] When you expand to portions of the property not worn out, broken, or deteriorated, you make an improvement.

Strategy 5–Repair after an event: Generally, you think about an improvement before you begin to make it.[18] There is usually a plan for improvements. With a repair, something happens that calls your attention to the need for the fix-up.[19] A broken water pipe requires a repair. Wear and tear produces the need to repaint. Events made it necessary to repair the pipe and paint the building.

 Sandy's elaboration: If you have an existing tenant, fix-ups can more readily be treated as repairs. If the tenant complains about something that needs fixing, this is the event that made the fix-up necessary. Document phone calls from tenants in your tax organizer, noting that they called your attention to a problem. If they sent you an e-mail, keep it in a file for that purpose.

Strategy 6–Repair during occupancy or between tenants: The IRS audit manual says you may buy a property, renovate it, and expense the costs.[20] The IRS tells its agents to watch for people like you and propose adjustments. You avoid some scrutiny when you own the property for a while before making repairs. Also, you fare better when you have tenants.

Major Case–Farmer's Creamery

This is one of the landmark cases in this area that really helps explain what you need to do in order to ensure that a fix-up is properly classified. This case will give you a feel for what you need to do in order to classify your fix-ups as repairs.

In this case, water seepage rotted the floor and walls of the building. Farmer's Creamery spent big dollars repairing the property. Because of the large repair costs, the IRS wanted the fix-ups to be classified as improvements. The tax court held that the fix-ups were repairs because:[21]

- The repairs were made for sanitary purposes, safety, and continued use of the building.
- The repairs were not part of an overall plan of improvement.
- The expenditures did not require a building permit. I assume that if a permit had been required, the court would perceive it as more akin to an improvement.
- The materials used to make the repairs were similar to the materials replaced.
- The repairs did not enlarge or change the building design. The company took pictures of the building before and after the repairs to show that there was no major change in the building design.
- The fix-ups did not prolong the building's useful life.
- It appeared that the company fixed only the deteriorated parts.
- The company properly classified the fix-ups as repairs in its records.
- The company replaced less than half of any wall, ceiling, or floor.

 Sandy's elaboration: Thus, the bean counters (accountants) placed the beans in the right spots.

Build a Strong Paper Trail with Good Records

To bulletproof your repair classification, keep receipts, document events that preceded repairs, and note the nature of the fix-ups in your log book. Your best proof may be a photograph. Take before and after pictures of the parts of the building undergoing repair. If they look alike, that suggests a repair. Make sure that you get a date stamp on the prints so that you can prove when you took the photos. Many digital cameras will do this.

Other Examples from the Courts

Think like a lawyer readying a case for repairs. You need evidence that supports your position. There are many gray areas in the definition of repairs. You certainly want rental property fix-ups to be properly classified as repairs. The courts reasoned that the following fix-ups were repairs:

- Timbers to support a sidewalk built over a basement[22]
- Copper sheeting to replace a cornice blown off by the wind [23]
- Straighten roof alignment because of sinking subsoil[24]
- Resurface a damaged floor, plastering, plumbing, and repairing glass[25]
- Line walls and basement floors to prevent further oil seepage[26]
- Tuck-pointing and cleaning exterior walls of a brick building[27]
- Paint and whitewash walls and ceilings[28]
- Replaster and repaint[29]
- Patch a leaking roof with similar materials[30]
- Shore up the building foundation to prevent collapse[31]
- Replace an air conditioning compressor[32]

Sandy's elaboration: Note that most items deemed repairs were linked to a cause. The cause could have been wind damage, water damage, or sinking subsoil. Improvements generally involve a plan, not a cause. Roof fix-ups have not been categorized clearly by courts. Some decisions allow for whole roof fix-ups to be repairs, yet other decisions would not allow fix-up of an entire roof to be a repair. The following have been held to be improvements:

- New doors for a building[33]
- New iron grills on windows[34]
- New fire escapes[35]
- New skylights[36]
- New oil-burning heating system replacement for coal burner[37]
- Lowering the basement floor to fit the basement for a new use[38]
- Replacing the entire side wall and front of a building[39]

- Substituting one type of window for another[40]
- Rewiring a building[41]
- Replacing wood floors with cement floors[42]
- Painting a house to make ready for a rental[43]
- Replacing office bookshelves with new built-in bookshelves[44]

 Hot tip: If you want your fix-ups to be classified as repairs, avoid the word "new." Instead, think of mending and restoring to the original condition.

Bottom Line

For rental or business property, you get far more from your repairs than from improvements. You can have more repairs if you pay attention to your records. Keep receipts to support all costs, whether they are repairs or improvements. Use logic that is supported by written evidence. If a pipe breaks, replacement is a repair. However, if you decide to replace the pipe before any intervening event occurs, it may be an improvement. Decide how you want to classify and gather your evidence accordingly.

Summary

- You get maximum tax benefits when you repair investment, commercial, or business property. You get maximum tax benefits for principal residences and second homes when you have an improvement.
- On rental or business property, repairs are immediately deductible subject to the passive loss rules. Improvements must be capitalized and depreciated over the life of the property, which is 27.5 years for residential rental property and 39 years for commercial and business property. No repairs are deductible on principal residences or second homes unless an office at home is claimed or the homes are rented out and deemed rental property.
- Repairs restore to a sound state and mend. They usually are preceded by an event such as a leakage, sinking subsoil, or wind damage. Tenants usually will call you because something occurred to cause a problem.
- Improvements usually involve a plan and result in a new item, rather than just fixing part of an item or a wall.
- Six strategies to help ensure classification as repairs are:

  1. Segregate repairs from improvements
  2. Fix a minor portion of a wall or roof–usually less than half
  3. Use similar, comparable, or less expensive materials unless such materials have proven to be ineffective

4. Fix the damaged portion only
5. Repair after an event and document the event in your tax organizer
6. Repair during occupancy or between tenants

- Avoid the word "new" when incurring fix-ups–you want to mend and restore.
- Use logic and keep a good paper trail.

Notes

1 Section 168 of the IRC
2 *Ibid*
3 Section 1.162-4 of the Regs
4 *Illinois Merchants Trust Company vs. Comm.*, 4 B.T.A. 103 (1926)
5 Sections 1.162-4 and 1.263(a)-1(b) of the Regs
6 For example, see *Munroe Land Company vs. Comm.*, 25 T.C.M. 3 (1966).
7 Section 1.263(a)-1(b) of the Regs
8 Section 1.162-4 of the Regs
9 *Jacobson vs. Comm.*, 47 T.C.M. 499 (1983). See also I. R.M. 4843.22
10 *Ibid*
11 *Allen vs. Comm.*, 15 T.C.M. 464 (1956) et al.
12 I.R.M> 4232.7 *Techniques Handbook for Specialized Industries-Construction,* Subparagraph 72 (18), Expensing of Capital Items
13 Section 1.162-4 of the Regs. See also *Ritter vs. Comm.*, 47-2 U.S.T.C. 9378 (6th Cir. 1947), which involved a new roof
14 *Abbot Worsted Mills, Inc. vs. Comm.*, 42-2 U.S.T.C. Paragraph 9694 (1942)
15 *Illinois Merchants Trust Company,* 4 B.T.A. 103 (1926)
16 See footnote 14
17 *Sanford Cotton Mills, Inc. vs. Comm.*, 14 B.T.A. 1210 (1929) (portion of decayed floor replaced)
18 *Jones vs. Comm.*, 24 T.C. 563 (1955), aff'd 47-1 U.S.T.C. Paragraph 9517 (5th Cir. 1957)
19 *J.F. Wilcox and Sons vs. Comm.*, 28 B.T.A. 878 (1933), Nonacq by IRS (broken glass replaced)
20 See footnote 12
21 *Farmer's Creamery Company vs. Comm.*, 14 T.C. 879 (1950), non-acq., 1954 C.B. 8
22 *Forgeus vs. Comm.*, 6 B.T.A. 291
23 *Commodore, Inc. vs. Comm.*, 46 B.T.A. 718 (1942), Aff'd 43-1 U.S.T.C. Paragraph 9362 (6th Cir. 1943)
24 *Gopcevic vs. Comm.*, 3 T.C.M. 1216 (1944)
25 *Rose vs. Haverty Furniture Company* 15 F.2d 345 (5th Cir. 1927)
26 *Midland Empire Pacing Company vs. Comm.*, 14 T.C. 635 (1950)
27 *City National Bank vs. Comm.*, 11 T.C.M. 411 (1952)
28 *Cohen vs. Comm.*, 7 T.C.M. 681 (1948)
29 *O'Madigan vs. Comm.*, 19 T.C.M. 1178 (1960), Aff'd 62-1 U.S.T.C. Par. 9332 (9th Cir. 1962)
30 *Pierce Estates, Inc. vs. Comm.*, 16 T.C. 1020 (1951), Rev'd on other points, 52-01 U.S.T.C. Par 9278 (3rd Cir. 1952)
31 *Illinois Merchant Trust Company vs. Comm.*, 4 B.T.A. 103 (1926)

32 *San Marco Shop, Inc. vs. Comm.*, 12 T.C.M. 843 (1953)

33 *Alabama-Georgia Syrup Company vs. Comm.*, 36 T.C. 747 (1961)

34 *The Fidelity Storage Corporation vs. Burnet*, 588 F.2d 526 (DC Cir.1932)

35 *RKO Theaters, Inc. vs. Comm.*, 58-2 U.S.T.C. Par. 9691 (Court of Claims 1958)

36 *St. Louis Mellable Casting Company vs. Comm.*, 9 B.T.A. 110 (1927)

37 *Bonwit Teller and Company*, 17 B.T.A. 1019 (1929), rev'd on other grounds

38 *Difco Laboratories, Inc. vs. Comm.*, 10 T.C. 660 (1948)

39 *Coca-Cola Bottling Works vs. Comm.*, 19 B.T.A. 1055 (1930)

40 *Acme Pie Company vs. Comm.*, 10 T.C.M. 97 (1951)

41 *Lycoming Silk Company vs. Comm.*,11 B.T.A. 523 (1928)

42 *Best vs. Comm.*, T.C. Memo 1954-170

43 *Pryor vs. Comm.*, T.C. Memo 1954-60

44 *Beaudry vs. Comm.*, 150 F.2d 20 (2nd Cir 1945)

Part 6

Minimizing Taxes when Disposing of Real Estate

Depending on whether the real estate is your principal residence, second home, or investment rental property, you have various choices for disposing of your property. For all types of property, you can sell it. The terms of sale will depend on negotiations with the buyer. You can have a sale for cash or you can receive payments over a period of time, using installment sale treatment for tax purposes. If it is investment or commercial property, you can enter into a tax-deferred exchange for other like-kind property and defer all or most of the gain on sale. All of these options present tax-planning opportunities and require proper handling by you in order to minimize the tax incurred. Part 6 covers these subjects.

23

How to Calculate Gain or Loss

The Eiffel Tower is the Empire State Building after taxes.

—Anonymous

Overview
1. Understand the process for determining gain or loss
2. Learn what comprises the amount realized for tax purposes

My goal is not to make you an accountant or to replace your accountant; however, you need to understand all the information here in order to appreciate what will be discussed in the remaining chapters.

Regardless of your choice for disposing of real estate property, the first thing you must do is calculate the amount of your gain or loss from the transaction. There are two elements to this process:[1]

- Determine the amount realized from the transaction
- Subtract the adjusted basis of the property from the amount realized

Step 1–Determining the Amount Realized from the Transaction

The amount realized from a transaction is sometimes thought of as the selling price. In most cases, the sales price is equal to the amount realized. However, tax law uses a different approach because you can dispose of property in transactions other than by sale (e.g., an exchange). Therefore, tax law doesn't look at the price tag attached to the property, but rather to what you get back from disposing of the property. This is the total of:[2]

- Cash you receive
- Fair market value of other property you receive in an exchange
- Liabilities you are relieved of because of the transaction (e.g., mortgage loans, unpaid real estate taxes)

Sandy's elaboration: The liabilities from which a taxpayer is relieved generally include liabilities paid, assumed, or taken subject to by the purchaser, regardless of whether a liability is related to the property or whether it is recourse or nonrecourse.

Step 2–Subtract Your Adjusted Basis

How basis is computed is discussed in Chapters 3 and 4.

Sandy's elaboration: Notice that the focus for figuring the amount realized on a sale is on what you receive rather than what you give up. If you are the buyer, your basis is focused on what you give up.

Example: Amy sells a rental home for $ 200,000. The terms of sale are that the buyer pays Amy $40,000 and assumes an existing $160,000 VA mortgage. The amount realized is $200,000. From the amount realized, Amy deducts her adjusted basis.

Adjusted Basis

As a reminder, your initial basis is generally your cost. This initial basis is reduced by any depreciation or casualty losses taken and increased by any improvements made.

Summary

- The formula for computing gain or loss is: the amount realized from the transaction minus the adjusted basis.
- The amount realized is usually the sales price, but it can be different if there is an exchange. The amount realized is the sum of:

  1. Cash received
  2. Fair market value of other property received
  3. Amount of liabilities relieved of because of the transaction

Notes

1 Section 1001 of the IRC
2 Section 1001(b) of the IRC and section 1.1001-2(a) of the Regs

24

When to Use Seller Financing

The invention of the teenager was a mistake. Once you identify a period of life in which people get to stay out late but don't have to pay taxes—naturally, no one wants to live any other way.

—Judith Martin (writing as Miss Manners)

I f you sell real estate for cash, you pay tax on all of the gain in the year of sale. Assuming you owned the property for at least a year, you pay tax at a maximum rate of 25 percent on any depreciation taken and generally 15 percent in federal tax for all other long-term capital gain above the depreciation taken. Wouldn't it be great if you could spread the gain over a period of years and earn money on the untaxed gain? Well, you can ... by seller financing, which involves taking back a note from the buyer.

Overview
1. Learn how to compute gain when there is seller financing
2. Understand why seller take-backs can create more wealth than selling for cash
3. Learn a great technique of the savvy rich: charge points with sell take-backs
4. Understand the tax consequences of repossession
5. Learn about the tax traps of seller financing with relatives
6. Learn why you should charge as little as possible for interest when seller financing
7. Learn the four circumstances when you should avoid seller financing

How Does Seller Financing Work?

As an alternative to a cash sale, you can use the installment method of reporting for tax purposes. This preserves capital gain treatment for the gain over the payment period. The key is that you pay a prorated share of the gain over the repayment period as you receive the cash. In this way, you get paid, and the government gets its share very slowly over a number of years. Installment sales reporting occurs when you receive at least one payment after the close of the tax year of disposition (sale).[1] It applies to any transaction in which payments are made in years after the year of sale. It applies when you take back a note, land contract, trust, etc.

Sandy's elaboration: The installment method only applies to your gains. If you have a loss on your investment or business property, you report the loss in the year of sale even if you get paid for the property over a period of years.[2]

In a seller carryback, you take back a note from the buyer; so you are financing the buyer. You get paid cash over time—such as from a 10-year second mortgage. You divide the second mortgage into three parts:[3]

- Interest
- Taxable profit
- Return of basis

Example: Amy sells her home for $200,000 with a $50,000 profit on the sale because her basis was $150,000. Her profit percentage is 25 percent ($50,000 profit/$200,000 selling price). If she receives a monthly payment of $1,300, of which $300 is interest, the $1,300 payment is treated as follows:

- $300 taxable interest, which is ordinary income
- $250 taxable profit, which is usually long-term capital gain
- $750 return of basis, which is tax free

Sandy's elaboration: Subsequent principal payments keep the same percentages of taxable and return of basis. This means that all succeeding year's payments will result in 25 percent of profit and 75 percent return of basis, after subtracting the interest from each payment. You pay tax on the profits, which are usually long-term capital gains, when you receive the cash. For accountants who are reading this: gain on the sale of property, which is subject to the installment rules, is reported on IRS Form 6252.

Every time you take back a note from the buyer, you automatically use the installment method of reporting your gain,[4] which means you report your gain in proportion to the principal received. This is automatic unless you elect out of installment reporting, as discussed below.

Advantages to a Seller Take-Back of a Note

Solid and Safe Profits

With a seller take-back of a note, you have a number of ways to increase your profits, including:

- Charging a rate of interest greater than you can earn from the bank or on money market accounts
- Charging more for the property because you are willing to take a note from the buyer
- Using the property as collateral in case of foreclosure provides you with safety for your take-back note (even in the worst scenario, you get your property back and keep the down payment plus other installments made)

Example: The bank pays 2.7 percent interest. Money markets pay 3 percent interest. Ten-year treasury bills might pay 6 percent. Today, you can earn up to 9 percent interest with a second mortgage. Assuming that you invest $100,000 at these interest rates, your cash accumulation after 10 years is:

- $130,528 in the bank
- $134,392 in a money market
- $179,186 in treasury bills
- $236,736 with a second mortgage

Can Increase the Chance of Selling the Property

When you are willing to finance a buyer with a second mortgage, you make it easier for them to get a first mortgage. In addition, they need less cash or less credit if you are financing the deal.

You get to collect the cash before you have to pay the taxes: When you finance your buyer with a seller take-back, you collect the cash and then pay the tax. The government gets paid very slowly over a number of years.

Example: Mary sells her home for $400,000; she paid $300,000 for it two years ago. She thus has a $100,000 profit in this example. She provides 100 percent financing for the buyer and receives a $40,000 down payment plus interest on the note for 10 years. In the first year, she collects $40,000 but only pays tax on $10,000 profit, which was computed by taking 10 percent of the profit because she received only 10 percent of the sales price.

More Principal Earning Interest

In a seller take-back, you earn interest on the note you take back. If you don't use a seller carryback, you earn interest on the residual that you have *after* paying the tax. The following example explains this.

Example: Matthew and Rachel sell their second home that has a cost basis of $250,000, which does not qualify for the exclusion, for $500,000. Consequently, they make $250,000 profit. Their gross profit percentage is 50 percent. If they sell the property for cash, they pay tax of $57,500 (assuming a 15 percent long-term capital gains rate plus 8 percent state rate). This leaves $442,500 to earn interest.

If Matthew and Rachel carryback a mortgage and receive a down payment of $50,000, they only include in income $25,000 (50 percent of the cash received, which is the gross profit percentage). They pay $5,750 in tax ($25,000 taxable income × 15 percent long-term capital gains rate plus approximately 8 percent state tax rate). This leaves them with $494,250 earning interest!

Lowers Your Tax Bite

The final advantage to providing seller financing in the form of a take-back note is that you may lower your overall tax bite. The IRS collects taxes in brackets. The higher your income, the higher your tax bracket. You can use the seller take-back to spread your taxable income over more years and keep yourself in a lower tax bracket.

The bottom line is that you have a lot of advantages when providing seller financing.

Hot tip–Charge points and increase your investment return: When you offer a second mortgage to a buyer, you allow the buyer to keep more cash. They can, therefore, buy the property with a lower down payment. Providing great terms is certainly enough reason for you to charge a point or two on the carryback of the note. With points, your investment returns can grow dramatically.

Example: Karen collects two points on a 30-year $30,000 second mortgage of 8 percent. First, the two points increase the effective interest rate from 8 percent to 8.44 percent. Second, if her buyer pays off the mortgage early, her earnings rise dramatically to 10 percent, 15 percent, maybe even as much as 19 percent (depending on how quickly her buyer refinances or pays off the second mortgage).

Structure the Deal to Multiply Profits If the Buyer Defaults

When you provide that second mortgage, you have to think "What will happen if the buyer doesn't pay?"

Repossession is not much of a tax problem for principal homes due to the exclusion rule; however, it is still a problem on sales of second homes, vacation homes, and sales of rental property.

Repossession Profit

Let's first make something clear: repossessing property sold using the installment method does not destroy the tax benefits. However, you probably will pay some tax on the repossession. Why? The reason is that you will have received some cash that was deemed to be nontaxable return of basis. If you get the property back, this untaxed amount becomes taxable. Repossession profit is based on the lesser of:[5]

- The untaxed portion of previous installments
- The total gain minus any previously reported gain and reacquisition expenses (legal fees, court costs, etc.)

Any remaining gain is untaxed until you sell the property. Further deferral is also possible if you resell using the installment method. An example should clarify some of this complexity:

Example: For $200,000 Elaine and Sol sell their property in which they have a basis of $40,000. They receive a $20,000 down payment and take back a 9 percent note for $180,000, payable in $20,000 installments over the next nine years. Their total profit on the sale is $160,000 ($200,000 contract price less $40,000 basis). Their gross profit percentage is 80 percent ($160,000 gross profit divided by the $200,000 contract price).

Sandy's elaboration: Gross profit percentage means the percentage of principal payment treated as capital gain. In our example, 80 percent of the principal is treated as capital gain.

If the buyer pays a total of $60,000, comprised of a $20,000 down payment and $40,000 in two installment payments, then defaults to Sol and Elaine, they repossess the property. The gain on repossession is the *lesser* of the untaxed portion of previous installments or the total gain minus expenses of repossession, which is computed as follows:

Step 1–Untaxed portion of previous installments:

Payments received to date:	$60,000
Portion of payments already taxed:	$48,000
Repossession gain:	$12,000

Step 2–Total gain minus both reacquisition expenses and previously reported gain:

Total gain:	$160,000
Gain already taxed:	$48,000
Untaxed gain:	$112,000

Thus, Elaine and Sol would only pay tax on the lesser of these two steps, which would be $12,000.

Repossession of Principal Residence

If the gain resulting from the initial installment sale of real property was not recognized because the property involved was the principal residence of the seller, and if the property is repossessed by the seller and resold within one year of the repossession, the provision requiring the recognition of gain on the repossession does not apply. No gain or loss is recognized by the seller as a result of the reacquisition of the property. Resale of the property within one year of the repossession is treated as a part of the transaction constituting the original sale of the property.[6] In addition, you can use the universal exclusion to shelter both the original gain and the gain from repossession if it involved your principal residence.

What Is the Basis of the Repossessed Property?

After repossession, the basis in the property is the same as when you sold it originally, plus any reacquisition costs.[7]

Example: Connie has an original basis of $200,000 in a property that she sold for $400,000 using the installment method. After recognizing gain on the repossession, her basis remains $200,000. If it costs her $2,000 to repossess the property, she adds the $2,000 to her original $200,000 basis for a new basis of $202,000.

Tax Planning Ideas for Creating Wealth with Seller Take-Backs

Lower the Interest Rate and Cut Your Taxes

With seller financing, most sellers try to get the highest interest rate possible without knowing this can be a bad idea.

Assume you sell your property for $150,000. The buyer pays $30,000 down and gives you a 10 percent fixed-rate 30-year mortgage on $120,000. Monthly payments are $1,053.09. If you keep the monthly payment and lower the interest rate to 7 percent over the 30-year mortgage, the principal increases to $158,286. If you make this change, you convert the $38,286.78 increase in principal from interest income to tax-favored long-term capital gains. You do this with no change in your cash flow or in the cash flow to the buyer from the transaction. You get $1,053.09 either way, but with the lower interest rate, you cut your taxes.

Sandy's elaboration: The key is to charge significantly less interest than what is considered the going rate. This way, you can raise the price and get more capital gains. The buyer gets a higher basis. If you are the seller, you might even be able to exempt more of your gain using the exclusion.

Example: Joan is going to sell her condominium (in which she has a basis of $100,000) for $200,000. She will avoid all the gain under the $250,000 Universal Exclusion. If she finances the buyer with a seller take-back note using interest that is a couple of points below the going rate, she may be able to ask a higher price. This results in no tax to Joan. She has converted interest, which is taxed as ordinary income rates, to long-term capital gain rates, which may even be completely tax-free under the Universal Exclusion.

Minimum interest rule: On an installment sale under $4,483,300 (indexed annually for inflation), you must charge interest at a rate of no less than the lower of:[8]

- 9 percent
- The applicable federal rate (short term, midterm, or long term, depending on the length of the seller take-back.[9])

Sandy's elaboration: You can find the applicable federal rate by going to www.irs.gov or by calling your accountant and asking her for the long-term applicable federal rate. As of the writing of this book, the applicable federal rate was 5.29 percent.[10] This changes frequently; thus, you need to know what the applicable federal long-term rate would be at the time that you institute the seller carryback note.

If you use a note whose maturity length is three years or less, use the federal short-term rate. If the note is from four to eight years, use the federal midterm rate. Finally, if the note is for nine years or longer, use the federal long-term rate. These rates, which change monthly, are found in the library, or you can ask an accountant for the latest numbers. In addition, there is a special exception for sale of land between family members. If you sell land under the installment method, there is a 6 percent maximum rate of interest that can be charged on the first $500,000 of sale proceeds.[11] Anything above $500,000 gets treated as any other sale. When dealing with relatives, if you have a sales price for land where the contract price exceeds $500,000, you may have two interest rates: one for the first $500,000 and one for the rest of the contract price, which is not subject to the 6 percent limitation.

Push the Sale to Next Year with an Escrow Account

In order to avoid any gain on the installment sale this year, you can use an escrow account for future payments. An escrow account will qualify for installment sale treatment provided the escrow meets three conditions:[12]

- The escrow agreement is part of an arm's length installment sale contract between you and the buyer, and

- You receive no present benefit from the escrow funds (such as monthly interest), and
- The escrow agent is not your exclusive agent

Sandy's elaboration: By using an escrow, you, in effect, guarantee both the down payment and/or next year's payment without being taxed on any portion of the money until the year after the payment. This gives you a one-year grace period before you have to pay tax.

Using an escrow works best when the closing is towards the end of the year.

Earn Tax-Free Interest by Combining the $250,000 Home Sale Exclusion with Seller Financing

When you want to take the $250,000/$500,000 exclusion but the house hasn't appreciated enough to take the whole exclusion, consider seller financing to increase your net worth. If your profit on sale would be less than the $250,000 (or $500,000 married filing jointly), you can use easy seller financing terms to increase the sale price of your home, thus increasing the gain that can be excluded. In addition, there are four other reasons to consider the great terms for seller financing:

- More interest income than a bank would pay the seller
- Lower interest rate than a bank would charge the buyer
- Secure investment
- You might be able to charge points

Example: Sue is a single taxpayer who may be selling her home for a $200,000 profit. If she were to provide seller financing, the normal rate, in her area, would be 9 percent interest. If instead she charges only 5 percent, she might be able to sell her home for a $250,000 profit; thus, making an extra $50,000 tax free as a result of the Universal Exclusion.

Potential Installment Sale Problems

There are situations that you need to be careful about or, in some cases, even avoid in using any seller financing.

Structuring Installment Sales to Relatives

If you sell depreciable property to certain relatives, and those relatives sell the property within two years after acquiring it from you, you must report as taxable income all deferred gain on the sale.[13] Yuck!

Relatives, for purposes of this section, include:

- Brothers
- Sisters
- Spouses
- Parents
- Grandparents
- Children
- Grandchildren

Example: Dad sells a rental property to his son under an installment contract for $500,000. Dad's profit is $200,000. He will report taxable income of $10,000 for each of the next 20 years as he collects annual payments of $25,000 ($200,000 profit over 20 years = $10,000 per year). However, the son, after paying one installment causing $10,000 of taxable income to Dad, pulls a big *no-no*! In the 14th month after the initial sale, the son resells the property to Nelson, not a relative. This will cause Dad to pay tax on the remaining $190,000, which is the remaining unrecognized profit even though dad won't receive all of the cash for 19 more years. Yuck!

Bottom line: If you use seller financing with a relative, make sure, in the agreement, that the relative cannot resell the property within two years of the original sale.

Other Related Parties

The "wait two years before resale rule" also applies to sales by you or from:

- Corporations in which you and your relatives directly or indirectly have 50 percent or more ownership, or
- An S corporation in which you own the stock, or
- Partnerships in which you have an interest, or
- Trusts that name you as a beneficiary, or
- Grantor trusts that treat you as the owner.

Use seller financing with nonrelatives: Under the installment sale rules, your relatives do not include your:

- Uncles
- Aunts
- Nephews
- Cousins
- In-laws

Sandy's elaboration: I have always told my wife that in-laws aren't relatives.

Excess Mortgage Trap

If you are subject to this trap, you should generally avoid using seller financing and not use the installment method. The excess mortgage trap occurs when a buyer assumes a debt that is greater than your adjusted basis. You might wonder, "How do we get a debt on property above our adjusted basis?" This might happen in several ways. First, you could have fully depreciated the property but did not completely pay off the debt. Also, you could have refinanced debt or even added debt due to the appreciation of your home.

The problem is that if your mortgage debt on the property that you are selling exceeds your adjusted basis, you are taxed on the difference regardless of the cash that you receive. You count this excess as taxable contract payment in the year of sale.[14]

Example: You sell a rental property for $600,000. You only get $60,000 as a down payment, and the buyer assumes your existing mortgage of $400,000. If your adjusted basis is $200,000, the $200,000 excess mortgage over basis ($400,000 mortgage – $200,000 basis) counts as a payment in the year of sale. This results in taxable income to you of $200,000 due to the excess mortgage and an extra $40,000 due to the down payment because two-thirds of your principal is capital gain ($400,000 gain/$600,000 sale price). Thus you are paying tax on $240,000 but only receive $60,000 in cash!

Planning tip: Most mortgages are not assumable today without permission by the bank. However, you might be able to avoid this problem with a wrap around mortgage.[15] In this arrangement, you sell the property subject to a new second mortgage that wraps around the first mortgage. The buyer makes wraparound mortgage payment to you, and you continue to make payments on your original mortgage payments.

Sandy's elaboration: As I noted, many mortgages do not allow sale of the property without trigging the old mortgage as due and payable. You certainly want to see a real estate lawyer in your state in order to ascertain whether this strategy will work. If it won't work in your state, you want to avoid seller financing if there is a large excess mortgage trap *unless* you get enough cash from the seller to pay the taxes due.

Trap on Installment Sales to 50 Percent or More Owned Entity

If you sell depreciable property on the installment basis to a 50 percent or more owned corporation, partnership, trust, etc., all gain on sale is recognized immediately as ordinary income and not capital gain.[16] Thus, sale to a related entity is a great way to convert favorable long-term capital gain to unfavorable ordinary income rates. This should ordinarily not be done unless there is another Code section that provides tax relief, such as the Universal Exclusion and your principal residence.

Recapture Disaster

An installment sale of property that involves depreciation recapture is a disaster. Thus, when can you have depreciation recapture? Generally, you have depreciation recapture to the extent that any accelerated depreciation you have taken exceeds the amount that you would have taken using the slower straight-line method of depreciation. This would only be the case for pre-1987 depreciation because the current depreciation system for real estate is based solely on straight-line.[17] If you have any accelerated depreciation on real estate before 1987, you would report all excess depreciation (difference between straight-line and accelerated depreciation) for residential property as ordinary income, which is entirely taxable in the year of sale, regardless of the cash that you received.[18] Ouch.

Thus, if you have a lot of accelerated depreciation taken, which means that you owned the property before 1987, you probably don't want to allow seller financing unless you get more than enough cash from the buyer to pay the taxes.

Forfeit of Passive Losses

If you remember our discussion concerning passive losses, noted in Chapter 18, real estate losses are allowed against any real estate gains. The problem is that if you have a lot of suspended losses and use the installment method, you won't be eligible to use all the losses because your gains are prorated over the period of time that you receive the payments. With seller financing and installment reporting, you pay the tax as you receive the cash. Thus, you might want to report all of the gain and free the losses. So you should keep the following rules in mind:

- When you completely dispose of a passive activity (such as sale of a building), you deduct all of your suspended passive losses on that activity.[19]
- If you completely dispose of a passive activity by using an installment sale, you deduct all suspended losses *to the extent that you report gain from the sale as taxable income.*[20]

Example: You collect 30 percent of the cash using seller financing and, therefore, recognize 30 percent of the profits as taxable income. You may deduct 30 percent of the suspended losses

Sandy's tip: You still can use seller financing and yet recognize 100 percent of the gain from the sale in order to trigger the suspended losses by electing out of installment reporting. This will allow you to use all suspended losses from the property to offset gains from its sale and not limit your passive loss carryovers to the percentage of cash received. In addition, if the suspended losses exceed the gain on the sale of the property, you can use any excess suspended losses against any other form of income[21] such as wages, pensions, capital gains, rents, etc.

How to Elect Out of Installment Reporting

The election, to be excluded from the installment method, must be made on or before the due date, including extensions, for filing your return for the year in which the sale is made.

To elect not to report a sale on the installment method, report the full amount of the gain on a timely filed return (including extensions), using Form 4797, Sales of Business Property, or on Schedule D of Form 1040, U.S. Individual Income Tax Return, or on Schedule D of Form 1120, U.S. Corporation Income Tax Return, whichever applies.

If the original return was filed on time without the election, and you realized, from this book, that you should have elected out of the installment method in order to use the suspended losses, I have good news for you. The election may nevertheless be made on an amended return that is filed no later than six months after the due date of the return, excluding extensions.[22]

Summary

- You must use installment sale reporting whenever you get a payment after the taxable year of sale. You may, however, elect out of installment reporting.
- Under the installment method, you recognize gain in proportion to the cash (principal) that you receive. Thus, if you receive 30 percent of the contract price, 30 percent of the gain would be recognized. Losses, however, are fully recognized in the year of sale.
- All payments consist of three parts: interest, return of capital, and capital gain. You first deduct the interest from the payment and then take your profit percentage from the remaining payment in figuring your capital gain. Your profit percentage is your profit divided by your contract price (usually sales price).
- There are a number of advantages to using seller financing on a property sale, including:

  1. You make solid profits and usually make higher interest rates than any bank or money market would pay you.
  2. It increases the chance of selling the property.
  3. You collect the cash before you pay the tax.
  4. You have more principal earning income. Essentially you are earning income on the tax money that you would have paid the government in an "all cash" deal.
  5. You can lower your tax bite because the gain is picked up over the years of the payment. You might be in a lower tax bracket in those years.

- Charging points in lieu of getting high interest might substantially increase your rate of return, especially when there is an early payment of your note.
- If you repossess the property, you pay tax on all the previously untaxed portions of your prior payments (i.e., those that were treated as return of capital).
- Your basis upon repossession is your original basis increased by any acquisition or repossession fees.
- If you repossess your principal residence and resell that residence within one year of repossession, the gain rules applicable to repossession don't apply. You simply take all the cash received from the original sale and the new sale and combine them for purposes of using the Universal Exclusion.
- Don't necessarily charge the highest interest rate that you can. Instead consider charging a much lower rate but increasing the price of the property in order to use more of the Universal Exclusion and to claim more capital gain instead of ordinary income on the interest.
- When using seller financing, you must charge the lower of 9 percent or the going federal rate for the same time frame as a similar note. Thus, notes of three years or less use the short-term federal rate. Notes of four to eight years

use the midterm federal rate. Notes of nine years in duration or longer use the long-term federal rate.

- You can defer gain for at least one year using an escrow account. However, you can't get any immediate benefit from the account, such as earning interest.
- If your house appreciation is not at least equal to the full $250,000/$500,000 of the Universal Exclusion, consider giving fabulous terms such as low down payment and low interest rates and raising the price to use more of the exclusion. This way, you convert interest, which is treated as ordinary income, into long-term capital gain.
- If you sell to a relative with seller financing, put in the note that the relative cannot resell the property within two years of sale or you will trigger all of the remaining gain.
- Either avoid installment reporting or at least get enough cash from the seller in the following situations:

  1. Avoid the excess mortgage trap, where the mortgage exceeds your basis
  2. Avoid sales to a 50 percent or more owned entity.
  3. Avoid recapture disaster for properties that you owned before 1987.
  4. Don't lose your passive losses. Consider electing out of installment reporting when you have a lot of suspended losses on the property. If you do elect out, make sure that your accountant files a timely election. If you should have elected out, consider filing an amended return.

Notes

1 Section 453(b)(1) of the IRC and IRS Publication 537, *Installment Sales (2004)*
2 Rev. Rul. 70-430, 1970-2 C.B. 51
3 Section 453© of the IRC and sections 15A.453-1(b)(2) of the Regs
4 Section 453(a) of the IRC
5 Section 1038(b) of the IRC. See also IRS Publication 537, *Installment Sales* (2004).
6 Section 1038 (e) of the IRC
7 Section 1038© of the IRC
8 Sections 483 and 1274 of the IRC. See also Rev. Rul. 2004-107, 2004-47 I.R.B. 852 (2005)
9 Section 1.1274-4(a)(2)
10 Rev. Rul. 2006-29
11 Section 483(e)(1) of the IRC
12 *Reed vs. Comm.*, 83-2 U.S.T.C. Par.9728 (1st Cir. 1983)
13 Sections 453 (e), 453(f)(1) and 318(a) of the IRC
14 Section 15A-453-1(b)(3)(i) of the IRC
15 *Professional Equities, Inc. vs. Comm.*, 83-2 U.S.T.C. Par. 9728 (1st Cir. 1983)
16 Section 453(g)(1) and 1239 of the IRC. However, gain can be reported on the installment basis if you can prove that tax avoidance was not a principal purpose for the sale. See section 453 (g)(2) of the IRC. However, the gain is still taxed as ordinary income unless excluded by some other section of the Code, such as the Universal Exclusion.

17 Section 168(b)(3)(A) of the IRC
18 Section 453(i) of the IRC
19 Section 469(g)(1) of the IRC
20 Section 469(g)(3) of the IRC
21 Section 453(d) of the IRC. See also Chapter 18 in this book.
22 Section 301-9100-2(b) of the Regs

25

How to Avoid All Gain on the Sale of Investment Property Using Like-Kind Exchanges

You must pay taxes. But there is no law that says that you gotta leave a tip.
—Advertisement

Overview
1. Learn how a like-kind exchange can avoid all real estate gain
2. Understand the steps needed to achieve a qualified exchange
3. Understand how to use the new deferred like-kind exchange
4. Learn who can be and can't be qualified as an intermediary
5. Learn about some of the latest tax planning techniques in order to equalize cash in order to avoid any gain

Normally, when you sell rental property, you pay tax on any gain. If you plan to buy other property, you use the leftover cash to make the new acquisition. You split the profit with the IRS and pay tax at a maximum rate of 25 percent on depreciation taken and 15 percent on capital gains above the depreciation.

The good news is that you don't need to split the profits with the IRS in the year of sale. Make the same deal with an exchange. In this way, you can put all the money, including the tax money that you would have paid, to work for you instead of in the IRS's pocket. In effect, it is an interest-free loan from Uncle Sam. Where else can you get an interest-free loan?

Example: Martha could sell her rental property but would pay $75,000 in federal taxes if she did. With an exchange, she puts off the $75,000 tax until she sells the replacement property. If she exchanges the acquired property, she may avoid tax on that too. In fact, if she keeps the property until her death, she and her beneficiaries avoid all gain accrued.[1]

 Sandy's elaboration: Dying to avoid gain is not one of my favorite tax planning tricks.

Benefits of a Like-Kind Exchange

The biggest benefit of a qualified like-kind exchange is that you pay zero tax in a transaction that rids you of your old property and puts you into a new property. In other words, the IRS lets you keep your tax money working for you while you own the replacement property.

In addition to paying zero tax—if this isn't enough—with property planning you can achieve other benefits:

- You can avoid recapture of depreciation. On an outright sale, you pay tax on depreciation taken at your normal tax rate up to a maximum rate of 25 percent. This is known as depreciation recapture. With a like-kind exchange, unlike that of installment sales, the recapture amount carries over to the new property. You don't pay tax on the recapture until you sell the new property.
- You can add more depreciation deduction. If you acquire a more expensive property with a like-kind exchange, you can boost your depreciation above what you were taking on the old property.
- You can increase your basis. If you take out a bigger loan or pay cash to acquire a more expensive property, you increase your basis in the new property, which reduces gain and increases deprecation.
- You might be able to make a more beneficial allocation between land and building. If you did not make a good allocation to the old building using an appraisal (as discussed in Chapter 19), you might be able to correct this problem by getting an appraisal on the newly acquired property and allocating more of the basis to the building.
- You might be able to turn nondepreciable property, such as land, into depreciable property with a good allocation of basis using an appraisal.

Many of the richest taxpayers use like-kind exchanges a lot. As you can see, it is something you should seriously consider using as much as possible.

Overview of an Exchange

Tax law requires you to pay no tax on a like-kind exchange.[2] It also states that you don't recognize loss in a like-kind exchange.[3]

If your property would produce a loss when sold, you don't want to have a like-kind exchange with it.

In order not to recognize gain in a like-kind exchange, you need to exchange your investment real estate for like-kind. The question is "What does like-kind mean?"

Like-kind means you can exchange investment real estate for either improved or unimproved property (such as raw land). You can even trade rental homes for apartment houses and vice versa. However, real estate is not like-kind with personal property such as automobiles, jewelry, or stocks. Generally, real property is like-kind to other real property.[4] The property must be held for investment or used in a trade or business. It cannot be dealer property (held primarily for sale) and *cannot be your principal residence.*

Sandy's elaboration: Note that the focus is on your use of the property. If you trade for someone's home because you want to make it a rental property, the home is a rental property in your hands. The trade qualifies for tax deferral.[5]

When you receive non-like-kind property, you are taxed on your realized gain up to the amount of non-like-kind property such as cash. To simplify matters, any non-like kind property received is called "boot," which stands for the Treasure Island term: booty.

Two Types of Exchanges

You can have two types of exchanges. The first type is where you exchange one property for another. The second and more common type is known as a deferred exchange. Here you exchange your property for cash, which is put in trust with a qualified intermediary. The trust then purchases the property or properties that you identify.

Players

To make an exchange, it is best to have four players:

- You
- Buyer for your existing property
- Seller of a property or properties that you want to acquire
- Agent or lawyer (intermediary) to hold the properties and the proceeds from the sale of your property

Sandy's tip: It is important to use an intermediary who understands and specializes in exchanges. Once you have the right intermediary, you need to find:

- Property or properties that you want to acquire
- A buyer

When you have chosen the property you want to acquire and you have a buyer for that property, have the intermediary conclude the exchange by:

- Identifying the property you want and securing bank financing if needed when the exchange occurs
- Transferring cash to your intermediary for the down payment if the cash supplied by the buyer was insufficient to acquire the new property
- Selling your investment property to the buyer under an agreement providing that all sales proceeds go to the intermediary as part of an exchange (instead of a contract for sale, you need an exchange agreement)
- Having an intermediary purchase the property you want to acquire with the proceeds obtained from the buyer of your property

Sandy's elaboration: Note that the proceeds from the sale of your current property go to the intermediary for acquisition of the property you want. All this can take place in a matter of minutes or over the period specified in the law. If everything is in place, the entire transaction can take less than 30 minutes in the intermediary's office.

Disqualified Persons

Congress put in place a lot of stupid rules as to who can and can't be a qualified intermediary. Your intermediary may *not* be a person who has acted as your employee, attorney, accountant, investment banker, broker, or real estate agent within the two-year period ending on the date of the transfer of relinquished property.[6]

Example: Susan wants to use her real estate attorney or accountant (both of whom she used a year-and-a-half ago in a real estate closing) to serve as financial intermediary in a 1031 exchange. Neither will qualify because she worked with both within two years of the proposed transfer.

A person is not disqualified for services with respect to any 1031 exchange for:[7]

- Routine financial, title insurance, escrow, or trust services by a financial institution, title insurance company, or escrow company

If you own 10 percent or more of the entity providing intermediary services, you are dealing with a disqualified person even if that entity is a financial institution or title insurance company.[8]

Example: Your accountant prepares your tax return every year. Your accountant is not a qualified intermediary.[9]

Example: You own 20 percent of a title company. Even though a title company can usually be a qualified intermediary, you can't use this title company because you own 10 percent or more of the company.

Deferred Like-Kind Exchange

There is an exchange known as a deferred like-kind exchange, which is otherwise known as a Starker exchange. These rules came into effect as a result of the Starker case.[10]

Under the Starker regulations, you may wait a period of time after your initial trade to identify and close on another property. You don't need to obtain a property at the time of the sale of your old property. What tax law requires is:[11]

1. Within 45 days of the transfer of the old property, you identify the property that you want in exchange
2. You have the new property transferred to you within 180 days or by the time the return is filed (including extensions) for the year in which transfer of the old property occurs, *whichever is earlier*

Avoiding Tax on the Exchange

If you want to avoid paying tax on the exchange, do not accept:

- Property that is not like-kind
- Cash (which is called "boot" in tax law—for the old Treasure Island term "booty")
- A reduction in your mortgage debt that would be more than the debt you assume with the new property

Treatment of Cash

Cash or other non-like-kind property received in an exchange is taxable to the extent of gain. You pay tax on the lesser of your gain (as if the property were sold outright) or the cash and other non-like-kind property received. You may deduct from the taxable cash expenses for lawyers, real estate commissions, consultants' fees, and closing costs.[12] However, if you have cash in your pocket after paying these expenses, the extra cash is taxable.

Example: Arlene transfers her investment property in a like-kind exchange. If she were to sell the property, her gain would be $200,000. If she receives $100,000 cash net after closing costs, she is taxed on the lesser of her net gain, as if the property were sold ($200,000), or her net cash after all closing costs are subtracted ($100,000). Her taxable income would be $100,000.

Mortgage Relief

Here is a real trap for the unwary. You treat mortgage relief as a payment of cash to you,[13] which is taxable to the extent that you would have had a taxable profit if the property were sold.

Sandy's elaboration: When I refer to mortgage relief, I am talking about the amount of mortgage on your old property and subtracting the amount of any new mortgage on the new property. If the amount of the old mortgage exceeds that of the new mortgage, you have boot (non-like-kind property) to the extent of the difference. If the amount of a new mortgage exceeds the amount of the old mortgage, you don't have any boot from mortgage relief.

Example: Jennifer transfers property with an $80,000 mortgage and acquires property with a $50,000 mortgage. Tax law treats the $30,000 difference in mortgage relief (old mortgage less new mortgage on the new property) as taxable boot to the extent of gain on the property as if it were sold.

Sandy's tip: The bottom line is that if you want to avoid tax on exchanges, you want:

- Zero cash above the closing costs
- Zero net mortgage relief

If cash is coming your way, you can require your exchange partner to make improvements to the new property and finance them with a second mortgage.

Example: Sam wants to have a tax-free exchange of his investment property for another property. He has an $80,000 mortgage on his current property and would take a $50,000 mortgage on the new property. If this happens, he will have $30,000 of mortgage relief. However, instead of recognizing gain on the $30,000 of mortgage relief, he could ask the seller of the new property to place a $30,000 improvement on the new property before the exchange. This would result in Sam having to obtain a new mortgage on the newly acquired property of $80,000, which would result in zero mortgage relief.

Caution: The IRS has not been consistent when it comes to making the equity or mortgages even. In the case of Garcia,[14] the tax court ruled that a mortgage could be placed on the property before the exchange to even the equities exchanged. The IRS acquiesced to the Garcia case, cited in a private letter ruling,[15] then later contradicted itself in another private letter ruling.[16]

Best bet: Rely on the Garcia case, but discuss it with your tax advisor.

Miscellaneous Rules that You Should Know

There are some additional rules that you need to know in order to protect yourself:

- You may not trade property located in the United States for property located outside the United States.[17]

- If you trade with a relative and the relative sells the property within two years of the trade, the original trade is taxable.[18] Make sure you have an agreement that the relative cannot resell, trade, or dispose of the property within two years of the original exchange with you.
- If you get into the naming of replacement property, you may name more than one property during the 45-day identification period.[19] You can give or receive multiple properties for your properties. You can name up to three replacement properties or more than three replacement properties if the total value of all the named properties does not exceed twice the value of the property or properties you relinquished. So much for tax simplification!
- You may earn interest on money in escrow during the exchange.[20]
- You may not use your regular attorney or accountant as the exchange facilitator.[21]

Bottom Line

The like-kind exchange is a perfect way to use tax money to diversify your rental property portfolio. Remember, you defer the tax until you sell the property you receive in the trade. Make sure you do not take too much cash or debt relief. Remember, cash and net debt relief can result in taxable profit and could negate the benefits of the trade.

Finally, to keep your side of the transaction simple, find a lawyer and accountant who understand exchanges to guide you. You can ask realtors who have participated in exchanges for some suggestions of experts who have the necessary knowledge.

Summary

- A like-kind exchange is a great way to buy other or more expensive investment real estate without paying tax on the transfer. In effect, you are using the government's money to help you acquire new, better, and even more real estate than you currently have.
- Like-kind exchanges only work with investment real estate located in the United States. It will not work on your principal residence or second home regardless of their location.
- Generally, all real property is like-kind. Therefore, you can exchange a building that you rent out for apartments, commercial property, and raw land. Personal property such as automobiles, jewelry, gold bars, and stock are not considered like-kind property.
- It is your use that is important. You can exchange your investment property for someone else's principal residence if you use the property that you receive for investment or commercial purposes.
- To make the exchange, use an independent qualified intermediary to facilitate.
- The intermediary can't be an employee, accountant, investment banker, broker, or real estate agent with whom you have dealt within the two-year period ending on the date of transfer of the first of the relinquished properties.
- You can have a deferred exchange without even knowing what property you want to acquire. If you have a buyer for your property, you can structure the deal for the buyer to pay cash to a qualified intermediary. You then have to identify which property or properties should be acquired by the intermediary within 45 days of the original transfer. You must close on the deal generally within 180 days of the transfer or by the time your tax return is filed for the year, whichever is earlier.
- To avoid all tax in a like-kind exchange, don't receive any cash and don't have any net mortgage relief above the mortgage you will incur on the new property.

Notes

1 Section 102(a) and 1014(a) of the IRC. I should note that the estate tax is scheduled to be eliminated in the year 2010. If you die in 2010, there is still no gain to

the estate or beneficiaries, but they inherit the property with the same basis as the deceased. If they die, however, before 2010, the property gets a full step up in basis to the full fair market value as of the date of death. Also, transfers made within one year of death may not get a step up in basis under section 1014 of the IRC. This is to avoid the situation where you would give property to a relative who is terminally ill in order to avoid all gain when you inherit the property back.

2 Section 1031 of the IRC

3 Section 1031 of the IRC

4 Section 1031 of the IRC and section 1.1031(a)-1 of the Regs. See also 1.1031(a)-2 of the Regs

5 Section 1031(a)(1) of the IRC

6 1.1031(k)-(1)(k) of the Regs

7 See footnote 6

8 Section 1.1031(K)—(1)(k)(4) and (5) of the Regs

9 Section 1.1031(k)-(1)(k)(5)(i) of the Regs

10 *Starker vs. U.S.*, 602 F.2d 1341 (9th Cir. 1979)

11 Section 1031(a)(3) of the IRC and Regs thereunder

12 Rev. Rul. 72-456, 1972-2 C.B. 468

13 Section 1031(d) of the IRC.

14 *Garcia vs. Comm.*, 80 T.C. 491 (1983), *Acq*, 1984-1 C.B. 1

15 Private Letter Ruling 8248039

16 PLR 8434015

17 Section 1031(h)(1) of the IRC

18 Section 1031(f)(1) of the IRC

19 1.1031(k)-(1)©(4) of the Regs

20 1.1031(K)-(1)(g)(5) of the Regs

21 Sections 1.1031(k)-(1)(g)(4) and 1.1031(k)-(1)(k)(2) of the Regs

26

Sales to Relatives

Worried about an IRS audit? Avoid what's called a red flag. That's something the IRS always looks for. For example, say you have some money left in your bank account after paying taxes. That's a red flag.

–Jay Leno

Overview
1. Learn why selling to relatives may eliminate your losses
2. Understand which relatives qualify for tax purposes

This chapter deals with a major tax trap: sales to relatives. If you sell to certain relatives at a loss, you will not be able to deduct the loss.[1]

Example: Carmen sells her rental property to her son for a $50,000 loss in order to give him a good deal. Because her son qualifies as a relative, she is not allowed to deduct the loss. Had she sold the same property to a nonrelative, she would be able to deduct a $50,000 loss.

Where Does the Loss Go?

The loss is transferred to the relative who purchases the property. Tax law simply does not recognize the sale of property to certain relatives at a loss. It's as if no sale took place.

When the relative sells the property to a third party at a profit, he or she may deduct the loss, but only to the extent that the sale to the third party produces a profit.[2]

Example: Carmen sells property to her son for a $50,000 loss, which is not deductible by Carmen. However, if her son sells the property for a $40,000 profit, he may take the loss to the extent of the gain. He can offset all of

181

the $40,000 profit. The remaining $10,000 of unused loss would be lost. Ugh!

What Happens If the Relative Sells the Property at a Loss?

If the relative's sale produces a loss (measuring the selling price against the price that the relative paid for the property), he or she may not claim any of the original loss. It is lost forever. Yes, you read correctly—the original loss is gone forever!

Example: Carmen sells her car to her son for $5,000 when her basis is $10,000. Carmen may not deduct the loss because she sold her car to a relative. If her son sells the car for $2,000, he may deduct only the additional loss incurred after his purchase. Carmen's original $5,000 loss is gone forever.

Hot tip: You rarely want to sell property at a loss to a relative. It is much better to sell that property to a third party.

Who Are Your Relatives?

You may have more than you think. For purposes of this law, your relatives are your:[3]

- Husband or wife
- Mother and father
- Grandmother and grandfather
- Sons and daughters
- Grandsons and granddaughters
- Brothers and sisters
- Corporations and partnerships if you or your above-noted relatives own 50 percent or more

Sandy's elaboration: Although Congress tried to think of everyone, they left out cousins and in-laws. Therefore, cousins and in-laws are not "tax" relatives (as I have been telling my wife for years).

Example: Dan paid $20,000 for his car. He depreciated it to $10,000 and sold it to his son for $5,000. Dan may not deduct his $5,000 loss. The son has the right to use his dad's loss.

If the son uses the car in his business and sells the car for:

- $4,000—He deducts a $1,000 loss (the additional loss incurred).
- $7,500—He reports zero profit (his $2,500 gain is offset by his dad's $5,000 loss).

- $11,500—He reports $1,500 profit ($5,000 of his $6,500 gain is offset by his dad's loss).

Planning tip: Never sell business or investment property at a loss to relatives.

Summary

- Losses incurred when selling to relatives are disallowed. They are useable by the relative.
- If the relative sells the property at a profit, the disallowed loss may be used only to the extent of the profit.
- If the property is sold for less than the relative pays for the property, he or she may deduct the additional loss incurred.
- Cousins and in-laws are not considered relatives for purposes of this rule.

Notes

1 Section 267 of the IRC
2 Section 267(d) of the IRC
3 Section 267(b) of the IRC

Part 7

Miscellaneous Real Estate Tax Considerations

Here we deal with vacation home rules, bed-and-breakfasts, mom-and-dad motels, and frequently asked questions.

27

Understanding Vacation Home and Second Home Rules

On my income tax [form] 1040 it says "Check this box if you are blind." I wanted to put a check mark about three inches away.

—Tom Lehrer

Whistle
W
hen you rent out property, it is considered rental property. That makes the rules applicable to investment property apply to you. If you live in the property as your personal residence, there is a different set of rules. The question becomes "What happens if you rent out your home but live in it part of the year?"

Renting out a home you use personally has some traps that you need to know about because that is exactly

Overview
1. Understand that personal use of rental property makes the vacation home rules applicable
2. Learn how the vacation home rules apply to both personal and business use
3. Learn how to determine the limit of personal use in order to retain rental property status
4. Learn about the two-week rental exception where you can receive rent for two weeks on a tax-free basis
5. Learn about traps and donations of use

what the vacation home rules address. If you have a vacation home, you may be limited from being able to take rental losses. If it is deemed a rental property, and not a vacation home, the vacation home rules won't limit your losses.[1] What this means is if you are trapped under the vacation home limitation, the amount of deductions generated by the property cannot exceed the income it produces. In other words, you can zero out your income from the property, but you cannot create a loss to offset income from other sources.[2]

Example: Rachel owns a home that she rents out for $6,000 a year to Matt. If the vacation home rules apply, she may take rental property deductions up to the $6,000 in rental income from the property. No rental property losses may be taken against other income.

What Happens to Disallowed Losses?

If the loss from the property exceeds its income, the excess is suspended and you *can* use it in a future year when the property produces taxable income. In that year, you may deduct from the current taxable income any additional loss that is carried forward indefinitely.[3]

- Individuals whose personal use and rental use are both significant year after year are likely to accumulate substantial amounts of unused losses. Consideration might be given to reducing personal use in some years so that the property will become a rental property and not subject to the vacation home limits in that year. In this way, it may be possible to use both current losses and unused past losses as offsets against ordinary income in that year. Although it is not certain that this will be immune from IRS challenge, the language of *Code Section 280A* appears to permit this treatment. No regulations covering this point have been issued. Of course, these losses are subject to the passive loss rules. Similarly, accumulated losses may be deductible against any gain on the sale of the unit, although there is no authority to support a deduction at that time.[4] Tax law defines a vacation home as a dwelling used for both:[5]
- Personal
- Rental

Sandy's elaboration: This broad definition does not confine the limitation on vacation property to only resort properties. Any dwelling unit that you use both personally and for rental purposes can get caught within the rules if you occupy it too long. The vacation home limits apply to individuals, trusts, estates, partnerships, and S corporations. These limits do not apply to corporations (other than S corporations).[6]

Keep Your Personal Use to the Legal Minimum

Deductions for your second home are limited when your personal use (or that of certain family members) exceeds the greater of:[7]

- 14 days
- 10 percent of the days rented

Example: Rachel rents her second home for 220 days a year. She uses the home personally for 22 days a year. Her second home qualifies as a rental property and she can take the losses on the home. If her personal use is 23 days, it is subject to the vacation home limits.

Dwelling Unit

A dwelling unit includes a house, apartment, condominium, mobile home, boat, and similar property.[8] To be a dwelling unit, it must have basic living accommodations, such as:[9]

- Sleeping space
- Toilet
- Cooking facilities

Sandy's elaboration: Interestingly, you may live in a dwelling unit if it qualifies as a hotel, motel, inn, or other similar establishment.[10] For example, if you are running a bed-and-breakfast that is rented to tourists or long-term boarders, presumably you may live there and not run afoul of the vacation home rules.[11]

Generally, don't rent to relatives: If you have any personal use of rental property, your losses can be limited under the vacation home limits. In fact, if you rent a second home to a relative, the days of occupancy by the relative are considered personal use by you.[12] For this purpose your relatives include your:[13]

- Mother and father
- Brothers and sisters
- Sons and daughters
- Grandchildren and grandparents
- Spouse

Example: Victor and Maureen rent their beach cottage to their daughter for one week. Even though she paid them fair rent, their daughter's rental counts as personal use by Victor and Maureen.

Exception: Like many things in life, there is an exception whereby you can rent to relatives and not be subject to the vacation limitations. You may count as rental property a unit you rent to a relative at fair market value if it is his or her principal residence.[14]

Example: Using the same facts as above, if Victor and Maureen rent a town home to their daughter at fair rent, they can treat the town home as that of any other rental property if their daughter uses it as her principal residence.

Sandy's elaboration: This exception to the general rule of not renting to relatives may apply to a number of situations. For example, instead of paying rent to a school dorm, you might buy a building where your son or daughter attends college and have him or her rent rooms to their friends. Thus, you might be able to claim the building as rental property.

Rent for Fewer than 15 days to Make Rental Income Tax Free

If you rent a property for less than 15 days in a year, the total income is tax free.[15]

Example: Heather lives in Atlanta during the Summer Olympics. If she rents her home to ABC Sports for $25,000 for the 14 days of the Olympics, the whole $25,000 is tax-free income. What a great country!

Repair Your Vacation Home to Produce Nonuse Days

You do not use your vacation home for personal purposes on any day when your principal purpose for use of the unit is for repair or maintenance.[16] Such days are not considered as personal use days but are deemed nonuse days, which means these days don't count as personal use for the vacation home limitation rules. You can count as a repair day any day that you spend substantially full-time repairing or maintaining your vacation home.[17]

Example: You arrive late Thursday evening after a long drive to prepare your cottage for the rental season. You eat Thursday dinner at the cottage. Friday and Saturday you work a normal work day getting the unit ready for rental. Your spouse helps, but spends most of the time relaxing. You depart Sunday shortly before noon. The IRS says that the principal purpose of your trip is maintenance.[18] Under tax rules, you do not count your Thursday to Sunday use as personal use.

Example: You own a mountain cabin that you rent for the summer season. You spend a week with family members who work substantially full-time on the cabin during the week. You spend 3 to 4 hours a day helping and the rest of the time on the lake fishing. The IRS says that the principal purpose of the week's stay is maintenance.[19] According to tax rules, you do not count the week as personal use.

Stay at Your Vacation Home during Business Trips

Business trips incurred while staying at your vacation home could be tax-deductible trips. Business trips include those when you attend business-related seminars and conventions, see business prospects, etc. A trip to spend a week vacationing in your vacation home produces no deductible expenses.

A trip to repair the vacation home produces nonuse days and deductible travel. Similarly, use of your vacation home for overnight lodging while on a business trip is business, not personal, use.[20] However—and here is the catch—any personal use on any part of the day nullifies the business use and makes the day one of personal use.[21] So if you are on a business trip and stay at your cottage, you do not fish on the lake.

Do Not Donate Use of Your Vacation Home to Charity

This is a costly mistake people make due to their ignorance of the rules. The IRS says that donation of vacation home use to a charity is personal use by the owner. It does not matter how much the ultimate user pays for the use of the vacation home.[22]

Example: You donate a week of vacation home use to your school's annual auction. No matter how much the successful bidder pays to spend a week at your vacation home, the IRS counts the week of donated use as personal use by you.

- You get no charitable contribution deduction for your donation of the vacation home use.
- The bidder gets no deduction because he or she is deemed to have paid only fair market value.

Avoid Swaps, Barters, Exchanges, and Deals that Increase Personal Use

Swaps and deals count as personal use of your vacation home for any days you:

- Allow a person to use your unit under a deal that lets you use another dwelling[23]
- Charge less than fair market value[24]

Example 1: You swap a week of vacation home use with Harvey. Harvey's use of your vacation home counts as personal use by you.

Example 2: You let your neighbor use your vacation home at 70 percent of the fair rent. Your neighbor's use counts as personal use by you.

Sandy's elaboration: When I was at the IRS, I heard about a very instructive story. Two neighbors were complaining about their lack of deductions on their principal residences. One suggested they move into the other's home and rent their homes back to each other. Thus, each could try to depreciate his residence because it was now rented to his neighbor. The IRS caught on that this was a swap and disallowed all rental property deductions.

Timeshares

A time-sharing arrangement is one under which two or more persons with an interest in a dwelling unit agree to exercise control over the unit for different periods during the taxable year.[25] Typically, several taxpayers each have right of control for one or two weeks during the year. The regulations treat each of the owners as having a continuing interest in the unit for the entire year, regardless of how the interest is treated under local law (rather than limiting each owner's interest to the part of the year during which he or she is entitled to control). The bad news is that personal use by any owner of a timeshare is attributed to each owner, although income and expenses remain individual items.[26]

Sandy's elaboration: The IRS made timeshares the kiss of death. Each is responsible for all of the other owners' use. If the other owners use their weeks personally and you own only one week of use, you are deemed to use the unit for 51 weeks of personal use!

Summary

- If you use a property for both rental and personal purposes for any time during the year, you may be subject to the vacation home limitations.
- To avoid the vacation home limits, your business use should be the greater of 10 percent or less of the days rented or 14 days. If your personal use is greater than this, your deductions will be limited to your rental income from the property.
- Unused deductions arising from the vacation home limitations are carried over indefinitely until you have sufficient income from the property to use the deductions.
- Vacation home rules apply to any unit that has sleeping space, toilet, and cooking facilities. Therefore, it may apply to more than a cottage; it can apply to house boats, condominiums, etc.
- If you rent a property for less than 15 days, you don't pay tax on any of the rent.
- Ordinarily, don't rent to relatives because any use by them is considered personal use by you. There is an exception to this rule—if your vacation home is their principal residence and they pay fair rent.
- You may repair your vacation home and not have that day counted as personal use even if you stay there during the repairs.
- Don't donate use of your vacation home to charities.
- Avoid swaps and deals that increase personal use.
- With timeshares, the other owners' personal use is attributable to you, so you will almost always be subject to the vacation home limitations.

Notes

1 Although the vacation home rules won't limit your losses, you still need to avoid the passive loss limitation rules as discussed in Chapter 18, Minimizing Passive Loss Problems.

2 *Russell vs. Commissioner*, T.C. Memo., 1994-96

3 Section 280 A©(5) of the IRC

4 Section 82.7, *Kleinrock's Analysis and Explanation* (2006)

5 Section 280A of the IRC

6 No inference is to be drawn from Code Section 280A in the case of a corporation as to whether expenses incurred for the maintenance of a residence are connected with

its trade or business. H.R. Rep. 658, 94th Cong., 1st Sess. 165 (1975); S. Rep. 938, 94th Cong., 2d Sess. 152 (1976).

7 Section 280A(d)(1) of the IRC

8 Section 280A(f)(1)(A) of the IRC

9 Proposed Reg 1.280A-1©

10 Section 280A(f)(1)(B) of the IRC

11 Section 1.280A-1©(2) of the Regs

12 Section 280A(d)(2)(A) of the IRC

13 Sections 280A(d)(2)(A) and 267(c)(4) of the IRC

14 Section 280A(d)(3)(A) of the IRC and Section 1.280A-1(e)(5)(iii)(B) of the Income Tax Regulations

15 Section 280A(g) of the IRC

16 Proposed Regulation 1.280A-1(e)(6)

17 *Ibid*

18 Proposed regulation 1.280A-1(e)(7), example 3

19 Section 1.280A-1(e) of the Regs

20 Section 280A(d)(2) of the IRC

21 Proposed Regulation 1.280A-1(e)(1)

22 Rev. Rul. 89-51, 1989-1 C.B. 89

23 Proposed Regulation 1.280-1(e)(1)(iii)

24 Proposed Regulation 1.280A—1(e)(1)(iv)

25 Proposed regulation 1.280A-3(f)(3)

26 Proposed regulation 1.280A-3(f)(6)

28

Tax Benefits of Owning Motels, Hotels, and Bed-and-Breakfasts

The proper avoidance of taxes is the only intellectual pursuit that still carries any reward.

—John Maynard Keynes, economist

This chapter deals with the two-week rental loophole, tax benefits of being classified as a hotel, and bed-and-breakfast establishments. It's not a complicated chapter, yet it contains golden nuggets of information.

Overview
1. Learn how to deduct rent incurred while on a business trip that you pay your kids or parents, yet have the rent be tax free to them
2. Understand the tax advantages of being classified as a hotel rather than a residential rental property
3. Learn how you can make almost any rental property a hotel

General Rule for "Mom-and-Dad" Hotels

Tax law says that rental of some or all of your home for less than 15 days is not a taxable event.[1] In such cases, you ignore the rental income and do not deduct rental expenses or depreciation.

Travel Rules

As noted in my other book, *Lower Your Taxes—BIG TIME*, and in my home study program entitled *Tax Strategies for Business Professionals*,[2] you are in travel status when you sleep away from home overnight during a business trip.[3] Once in travel status, you may deduct 50 percent of your meals and 100 percent of your daily lodging as well as other expenses for each business day.[4] There is no requirement that you get lodging at commercial establishments.

Example: You spend 14 days working in the city where your parents live. If you stayed at a hotel with furnishings similar to your parents' guest quarters, you would pay $135 a night. If you pay your parents $135 a night for 14 nights ($1,890), you could deduct the full $1,890. The tax effect to your parents would be:

- $1,890 cash
- Zero taxable income
- Zero rental property deductions

IRS Compliance

When you pay more than $600 rent to an individual, the IRS requires that you report it on Form 1099.[5] Mom and dad report the gross rental income on Schedule E, which ties into Form 1099. They claim an offsetting deduction

as a miscellaneous expense on Schedule E and reference it to a supporting schedule stating "Taxpayers rented our personal residence for less than 15 days." Under IRC section 280A, taxpayers report no rental expenses and deduct as nontaxable the rental receipts of $1,890.

Document Fair Rent

Pay by check, even if it is between family members. Have mom and dad make a receipt for the payment. Make sure you pay fair rent—not too much and not too little. Document motel rates for quarters similar to those that you rent from mom and dad. Keep in mind that the IRS likes to examine family transactions.

Sandy's elaboration: This endeavor can be duplicated with your children. My parents were antique dealers. They used to visit me when I was in law school and stay at my apartment. They paid me rent for one week, which was tax free to me. They deducted the rent paid because they were on a business trip looking for antiques.

Hotel Tax Advantages

Rental property has potential tax traps. However, there are some advantages to having your rental property classified as a one-unit hotel. These include:

- No passive loss limits—all losses are fully deductible as business losses
- Easier and earlier recognition of a hotel as a business

Hotel Businesses Report Losses on Schedule C[6]

Unlike that of residential rental property, a loss from a hotel business reduces Social Security and Medicare taxes for sole proprietors and independent contractors. In addition, you can deduct all hotel losses against any other form of income because it is treated as a business loss.

Downsides of Being Classified as a Hotel

Although it is very nice to be immune from the passive loss limits, there are two negatives to being classified as a hotel:

1. Hotel depreciation: Hotels are considered commercial property that has 39-year depreciation.[7] This should be compared to residential rental property, which has a 27.5-year recovery period.

2. Hotels may be subject to Social Security: The IRS regulations specifically provide that where the landlord renders services such as maid service to occupants, the rent is Subject to Social Security.[8] Rents from hotels, motels, tourist camps, parking lots, warehouses, bed-and-breakfasts, and storage garages are generally subject to social security taxes. However, some services are not considered substantial enough to make the rent subject to Social Security taxes. The services you can provide include:

- Heat and light
- Cleaning of public areas
- Vending machines
- Trash collection

What Is a Hotel?

Your single-family home is a one unit-hotel when:

- Average customer stays are for seven days or less[9]
- You do substantially all the work to care for, rent, and account for the property.[10] In other words, you materially participate in the running and management of your property.

There is an exception where you can take business losses arising from real estate if:[11]

- The average customer stays for 30 days or less
- Significant personal services are provided. (If the value of the service is less than 10 percent of the rent paid, it is not considered attributable to the amount charged for the use of the property and is not a significant personal service.[12])

Sandy's elaboration: Examples of the second exception are a bed-and-breakfast, dormitory use by a student in a boarding school, and hospice care.

Zero Personal Use

If you use the rental for even one day of personal use, you lose the hotel classification.[13] Therefore, staying at your cottage and fishing would negate your hotel classification. You may, however, stay at a bed-and-breakfast if you are making breakfast for your tenants or personally providing maid service daily.

Worker Rule

The material participation rules discussed in an earlier chapter also apply in determining your qualification for hotel status. If you have someone help you with your hotel units, you must work:[14]

- More than 100 hours, and
- No fewer hours than anyone else works

Bottom Line

As good as hotel classification can be, usually rental property classification is better.

Summary

- Rental of a property for less than 15 days results in tax-free income to the recipient. If the person paying the rent is traveling on business, he or she may be able to deduct the payments.
- When going on a business trip, consider staying with your kids or parents and paying them rent for up to 14 days.
- Payments of $600 or more require you to send the recipient a Form 1099.
- Always pay by check and get a receipt.
- An advantage of being able to classify rental property as a hotel is that you can deduct all losses against any other form of income. Hotels are not subject to the passive loss rules.
- Two disadvantages of hotel classification are that you have a longer depreciation period and you have to pay Social Security.
- Your property is considered a hotel when the average customer stay is seven days or less, you do substantially all of the work to care for the property, and you render substantial personal services such as providing food or maid service.
- Be careful not to have any days of personal use by you other than what is needed to care for the property.

Notes

1 Section 280A(g)(2) of the IRC
2 *Tax Strategies for Business Professionals* and *Lower Your Taxes—BIG TIME* are available on my Web site at www.taxreductioninstitute.com. You can also obtain *Lower Your Taxes—BIG TIME* at most major book retailers, including Amazon.com, Barnes and Noble., and Borders Books.

3 Rev.Rul. 54-497, 1954-2 C.B. 75, 78, superseded in part by Rev. Rul. 75-432, 1975-2 C.B. 60 and modified by Rev. Rul. 63-145, 1963-2 C.B. 86, and Rev. Rul 75-169, 1975-1 C.B. 59, and Rev.Rul. 76-453,1976-2 C.B. 86

4 Section 1.162-2(a) of the regulations

5 Section 6041(a) of the IRC

6 IRS Publication 334, *Tax Guide for Small Business*

7 Section 168©(1) of the IRC

8 Section 1.1402(a)-4(c)(2) of the regulations

9 Section 1.469-1T(e)(3)(ii)(A) of the regulations. See also IRS Publication 925, *Passive Activity and At-Risk Rules* (2004)

10 Section 1. 469-1T(a)(2), and 1.469-1T(e)(3) of the regulations

11 Section1. 469-1T(e)(3) of the regulations

12 See footnote 10

13 *Byers vs. Comm.*, 82 T.C. 919 (1984)

14 *Ibid*

29

Frequently Asked Questions

Read my lips, no new taxes.
–George Bush

I have no intention of raising taxes.
–Bill Clinton

This chapter addresses some of the more salient questions that you, my cherished readers, have asked. The material will evolve as questions are sent to my Web site. I will answer them in future editions of this book if they are relevant to a number of other people. To submit your question, go to my Web site at www.taxreductioninstitute.com.

I am not giving specific tax advice in this book. Every situation is a bit different. Even slight changes in facts can make a big difference in the advice a tax professional gives. Therefore, all information you intend to implement should be checked out with your tax advisor.

1. I was told that if I am a real estate professional, I can deduct all of my real estate losses against any form of income without having to worry about the passive loss rules and without having to manage the properties myself. Is that true?

Response: I will give you a clear-cut answer: it depends. How's that for being clear-cut? A real estate professional is one who works a minimum of 750 hours in real estate trades or businesses, and at least 50 percent of his or her work time is in real estate trades or businesses. If you are a qualified real estate professional, you can avoid the passive loss rules and use all real estate losses against any other form of income without limitation. There is, however, one other requirement: either you or your spouse must materially participate in the management of your property.

If you hire a manager to run your rental properties, you will *not* meet this exception to the passive loss limits. You or your spouse must personally manage your real estate investments. For a more in-depth discussion, read Chapter 18.

2. You talk about deducting trips involved in taking care of my existing properties. May I deduct caretaking trips to timeshares?

Response: This is a great question. Yes, you can deduct trips to check out your investment properties as many times a year as is reasonably necessary. The IRS, having the most Scrooge-like folks around, allows two trips per year to take care of properties, absent some other special reasons such as checking for hurricane damage.

Timeshares, however, are treated differently. With timeshares, your use is tainted by personal use of the other owners. You cannot deduct caretaking trips to check out timeshares. However, your timeshare may qualify as a second home. If it does, you can deduct the interest and taxes incurred on the timeshare.

3. How should I take title to my real estate? Should I own it individually, through a Limited Liability Company, or in corporate name?

Response: This is one of the most frequently asked questions by seminar participants. Real estate generates depreciation and other deductions that flow through to the owner. It is for this reason that I don't recommend that you take title to real estate in corporate name. The reason is that the real estate losses generated will only benefit the corporation and not flow through to your tax return as well as if it were owned by you individually. Moreover, forming a corporation is like marriage: it is easier to get into and much harder to get out of. Getting real estate out of a corporation can be a taxable event.

As for owning real estate in an LLC, I have been recommending that for years—especially if it is a sole-owner LLC. Sole-owner LLCs are treated as if you own the property in your name. All the losses will flow through to you. In addition, you get limited liability for the property because the property is owned by the LLC. If liability is an important issue to you, you may want to own each piece of real estate in a separate LLC. This way, if there is a lawsuit concerning one of the properties, the other properties are protected. You can take title as a multiple-owner LLC as well. You are treated as a partnership for tax purposes, but you benefit from the liability protection of the LLC.

If liability is not an important issue, you can take title either jointly, as tenants by the entirety, or as tenants in common. What's the difference?

Joint ownership is when two or more people own property. If one dies, the decedent's share automatically goes to the remaining owners. There is no probate, which is one of the benefits of joint ownership. Joint ownership with family members, domestic partners, and significant others might be a good idea. However, be aware that it usually doesn't limit liability as well as if the property were owned by an LLC. Joint ownership doesn't avoid estate taxes. Generally, the decedent's share of the jointly owned property is included in the estate for estate tax purposes.

A tenant by the entirety is a form of joint ownership by husband and wife. The advantage is that in many states, property owned as tenants by entirety is protected from liabilities—if one spouse has a judgment against him or her, the judgment may not be used against property owned as tenants by entirety. One problem is that when one spouse dies, any judgment on the property or against the remaining spouse can now be enforced against the property. Yuck!

Another type of ownership is tenants in common. Your heirs inherit your share of the property. As a tenant in common, your will determines who gets your share of the property. There is no liability protection, however. This type of ownership is frequently seen with people who are living together. When one dies, his or her heirs inherit the deceased owner's interest.

For a more detailed discussion about the benefits of different types of entities such as corporations, limited partnerships, and LLCs, check out my bestseller entitled *Lower Your Taxes—BIG TIME*, which is available at www.taxreductioninstitute.com, www.amazon.com, Barnes and Noble, and Border's Books.

4. I was told that I should own real estate in my pension plan or IRA. How do you feel about this?

Response: If you ask this question of several accountants or tax lawyers, you will probably get several opinions. There are some unclear areas concerning property ownerships within IRAs and pension plans, and there is a lot of uncertainty.

I don't recommend owning real estate in pension plans for these reasons:

a. Lack of flow through of tax benefits: Real estate generates a lot of tax benefits through depreciation. However, if it is owned in a pension or profit-sharing plan, these benefits will not be useable. They will be locked into the plan, which can't use these benefits. Therefore, they are simply lost!

b. Pension and IRA distributions must begin within one year of your becoming 70 and 1/2: At some point, you must start distributing the property owned by the IRA or pension. You will be taxed on the distribution unless you own the property in a Roth IRA. You could be taxed on the full fair market value of the property without the cash available to pay the tax on the distribution. This could be a disaster. Yes, you could always sell the real estate; however, if the market is weak in the year of the distribution, you could be forced to sell for less than you would have gotten if you had waited.

c. Lack of leverage: Generally, real estate owned in pension plans and IRAs must be debt free. You might have transaction penalties. You might not be able to get one of the major benefits of real estate: leverage. Some authors contend that real estate may be owned in pension plans with debt on the property if planned correctly.[1] Frankly, it isn't clear whether you can do this without penalty. This is one of those things you should discuss with a tax advisor.

5. What tax return software would you recommend for me if I own some investment property?

Response: This may surprise you, but I highly recommend that you don't do your own tax return. I can't imagine why anyone would be so idiotic as to do that! The IRS has found that people who do their own tax returns have 11 times the error rate when compared to returns prepared by professional accountants. It is for this reason that doing your own return significantly increases your chance of being audited. Most tax software is quite good, but you almost need the knowledge of an accountant to use them properly. It's the old saw "garbage in—garbage out." Even I, as a tax writer and CPA, don't do my own tax return.

I have found that those who do their own tax return usually don't have the right support if they get audited. When an accountant does a return, he or she usually has a very comprehensive file that can be used for audits to make the audits go more quickly and easily.

Finally, if there is an error on the return caused by the preparer, you can sue the preparer and get your penalties and interest reimbursed. If you do the return yourself, you are stuck with your own mistakes. Consequently, you should not use relatives or close friends to do your return unless you are willing to sue them for mistakes.

6. What are the tax effects of giving options on real estate? There seem to be a lot of real estate gurus advocating the use of options to buy real estate.

Response: An option is the right for someone to buy property at a fixed price within a set time frame. An example of an option would be for me to give you the right to buy my home for $1.2 million if exercised within a one-year period from the date of the grant of the option.

To get an option such as this, you would have to pay me some money (consideration) in order to lock in my property at a fixed price. The money that you pay me for the option is the *option premium*. The price at which you can buy my home, which in this example is $1.2 million, is called the *exercise price*. Thus, when dealing with options, you have a premium or consideration for the option, an exercise price, and a time period after which the option expires.

In addition, there are two terms that you need to know. The *grantor* is the person giving the option, and the *grantee* is the person getting the option. Thus, in the above example, I would be the grantor because the option that is being given is on my house. The person paying me the premium and receiving the option is the grantee.

Sandy's elaboration: I really do wonder how business is able to get conducted in this country with all these confusing names and classifications that we have to understand.

There are several things that can happen with options:

a. No exercise is made of the option and it doesn't expire: During the term of the option and when the option is given, there are no tax consequences to both the grantor and the grantee.[2] Thus, at first the grantor doesn't pick up any income on the option premium and the grantee, who, if you remember, is the person paying the premium, doesn't get a deduction.

b. The option is exercised: If, however, the grantee exercises the option and does purchase my property, I would add the option premium to the exercise price and that would be my amount realized. Thus, if I received $10,000 for a premium to sell my home for $1,200,000, and the option is exercised, my total amount realized would be $1,210,000. Notice that the option premium is treated as part of the sale price. The grantee's basis on the property becomes the exercise price plus the amount of the premium.[3]

c. The option lapses: Questions often arise as to the tax consequences of the option premium if the option isn't exercised. The grantor picks up the premium as income in the year that the option lapses. The grantee takes a deduction as a loss in that year as well if the option was to be used on investment real estate. If it were placed on property that the grantee was going to use as his or her home, the loss isn't deductible.

Example: Pam offers me an option with a premium of $10,000 to sell my rental townhouse for $600,000 if exercised within one year in July of 2006. If the option expires in July of 2007 without being exercised, I have to pick up the $10,000 as income in 2007, not in the year 2006. Pam can take a loss on the option of $10,000 in 2007 if she were planning to use the townhouse as an investment. If she were going to move into the townhouse in order to make it her principal residence, she may not deduct the $10,000.

7. What do you do if you are buying a home for more than $1,000,000?

Response: The following tax planning strategy has been used by the superrich for years. Here is what they do:

- Limit your initial acquisition debt to $1,000,000: This means that you would have to liquidate enough stocks, bonds, and money markets so that your acquisition debt does not exceed $1,000,000.
- Wait 91 days after the closing: IRS has a rule[12] that states that any debt incurred for acquisition of the home within 90 days of the closing will be treated as acquisition debt. Thus, you want to wait at least 91 days after the closing to institute the next step.
- Refinance your equity after waiting the 91 days from closing: Refinance your home to take out the funds that you put into the purchase and buy back your investments such as stocks, bonds, mutual funds etc.
- Document where the refinanced proceeds went: You should certainly document where the money went. If you buy investments with the money, all interest on this debt becomes investment interest!

 Sandy's elaboration: You now can deduct the investment interest against any investment gains. If such interest exceeds such gains, you can carry them forward to future years indefinitely. Notice that if you incurred more than $1,000,000 of acquisition debt, all the interest above that amount (other than the home equity debt) becomes nondeductible and useless. You would get no carryover and no benefit.

Notes

1 E.g. *IRA Wealth, Revolutionary IRA Strategies for Real Estate Investment*, Patrick W. Rice and Jennifer Dirks, published by Square One Finance Guides (2003)
2 *Virginia Iron, Coal and Coke vs. Comm.*, 39 BTA 195, Aff'd. 89 F.2d 919 (1938)
3 Section 1234 of the IRC
4 Section 1, 163–8T of the Income Tax Regulations and IRS Notice 88–74, 1988-2 C.B. 385

Appendix 1

Recommended Tax Resources

I just wanted to present some other resources for you to improve your knowledge and put as much money in your pockets as possible:

1. Check out my Web site at www.taxreductioninstitute.com This site has been discussed in *Newsweek* magazine and also mentioned in many other journals. I have written articles for a number of publications. I always put copies of my articles on my Web site. It has a number of great articles on various topics. In addition, there are question-answer forums hosted by other accountants. You might also like to check out my article entitled, "Life Lessons," which is my version of *Chicken Soup for the Business Soul*. Also, there are some terrific products such as my home study course "Tax Strategies for Business Professionals," and "Unlimited Consulting," where you can get your tax questions answered. There are even recommended tax preparation services, audit protection services, and much more.

2. Get the book *Lower Your Taxes—BIG TIME*. This was my first best-selling book. It contains a wealth of information not found in this book on small business and home-based business. Remember, real estate investment is a form of business, and most of the information found in that book can also be used in investment properties. My book can be found where you got this book or on my Web site, on Amazon.com, or in many other fine book retailers.

3. Have you ever wondered if there is a way for you to keep track of all your automobile mileage, entertainment, and travel questions, and do all this by simple dictation? Well, fret no longer. There is a way to send out e-mails, keep track of all tax mileage and logs, keep online to do's and appointments, and much more. In fact, you will soon be able to

have your e-mails read to you and dictated back as well! There is some amazing technology now available to you. To find out more, go to: www.evaforhire.com and use sponsor number 10297 to access the site.

4. Go to www.irs.gov and http://www.irs.gov/businesses/small/. These are various IRS Web sites. Lots of good information can be found here, especially in the IRS publications. The only problem with IRS publications is that although they may be somewhat clear, they are very boringly written. The IRS hasn't gotten the hint yet that tax writing should be made interesting as well as clear.

5. Check out the Jackson-Hewett tax Web site at: http://www.jackson-hewitt.com/resources.asp. They have some interesting tax articles and tips as well. They even have a nice tax calculator.

6. H and R Block has a great Web site for tax resources, which can be found at: http://www.taxcut.com/taxtips/taxresources.html. They have a tax estimator, withholding calculator, and articles on tax law changes and tax tips. It is a very useful Web site.

7. For various state and local tax information for all 50 states, go to: http://www.taxsites.com/state.html.

8. Although I don't recommend doing your own tax return, Intuit does have a useful site with lots of tips. You can get this information by going to: http://www.turbotax.com/tax_tips_and_resources/.

9. If you have international tax questions, you might want to try out this site: http://www.taxworld.org/OtherSites/International/international.htm.

10. Did you ever wonder where you can find IRS regulations or where you can find information in estate planning or in proposed tax bills? Well, wonder no longer. *Tax Advisor* magazine has a great site with links to other tax-related sites. They even have amortization calculators. You can get there by going to: http://www.investmentadvisor.com/issues/2005_11/special_report/5554-1.html.

11. Sagefire International has a great online shoebox/diary for anyone in small business and for real estate investors. It's a great online tool for use with my tax organizer/diary found on my Web site. Sagefire has business coaching, a payroll service, and even does tax returns. You can access Sagefire by going to: www.sagefire.com/tax.

12. Monster.com has more than just job listings. They have lots of information on relevant IRS forms and publications for small businesses. You can access them by going to: http://ct.monster.com/articles/taxforms/.

13. If you are a stock or commodities trader, you might want to go to: http://www.edaytradertax.com/ and http://www.tradersaccounting.com/a_trader.asp.

14. About.com has good tax resources and articles. You can access them by going to: http://credit.about.com/library/weekly/aa021601a.htm.

15. The American Bar Association Web site has a lot of technical information such as the Internal Revenue Code, regulations, links to IRS forms and publications etc. To access them, go to: http://www.abanet.org/tax/sites.html.

16. If you want information on incorporating in most states, including Nevada, check out: http://www.nvinc.com/. If you are just interested in incorporating just in Nevada, check out: http://www.laughlinusa.com/.

17. Although this site doesn't deal much in tax planning, it has some of the best financial calculators around. If you want to see how much money you need to save for college, retirement, or what you need to pay in order to retire a debt early and much more, go to: http://www.fincalc.com/. For more investment related calculators go to Kiplinger's Web site at: http://www.kiplinger.com/personalfinance/tools/investing/index.html#funds.

18. For information on financial coaching and money management, one of the best sites around is the Money Management site, which you can access here: http://www.moneymastery.com/.

19. You should also consider obtaining their book, *Money Mastery, 10 Financial Principles That Will Change Your Financial Life Forever*, by Alan Williams and others. It is a well-written treatise on how to manage money and what it realistically takes to be a millionaire. In fact, if you follow their advice, and give yourself at least 20 years, you will probably easily achieve millionaire status, not counting the equity in your home. You can get their book by either going to the Money Mastery Web site, noted in item 18, or going to Amazon.com or Barnes and Noble.

20. There are many people selling tax fraud schemes. Hucksters are promoting a variety of bogus arguments as to why you don't need to pay taxes, or they suggest setting up phony offshore trusts to allegedly avoid all taxes, etc. Fortunately, the Financial and Tax Fraud Education Associates provide a good Web site that notes those who have been indicted or convicted of selling tax fraud schemes. You can access their site here: http://www.quatloos.com/.

Appendix 2

Leveraging Today's Technology

Using Technology to Help You with Your Real Estate Investment

Overview
1. Using technology to help you with your real estate investment
2. The simple rule of good versus bad technology
3. Beware of the "get rich fast" technology solutions
4. Benefits of online Internet applications
5. Understanding and minimizing Internet security risks

In today's environment, no book would be complete without at least a state-of-the-market on technology. For real estate investors, technology purchased for your real estate investment business, besides being a valid tax deduction, will help to simplify, automate, and back up the required record keeping and administration for your investment. Remember, Uncle Sam (a.k.a. the real estate bookie) is particular about having your investment documentation complete, in good form, and available for him to review for up to four years. All purchase documents are viewable for as long as you own the property and for four years after you have a taxable sale. Technology, when used properly, saves us countless hours of work, as well as a lot of headaches. The trick is to use technology's strengths: it is particularly good at capturing and organizing information and then storing that information for long periods of time.

The Simple Rule of Good versus Bad Technology

Technology (and software in particular) has created great efficiencies and productivity for all of us. Consumers can research products, health care

213

issues, and the latest news over the Internet faster than ever. Businesses can do their job functions easier, faster, and better. Investors can track their investments and back up their data daily. However, the dirty little secret about technology is that there have been poor technologies released that promised castles in the sky but never worked. These empty promises consumed millions of dollars and hours of time but never provided anything useful.

So how do you find the good technology and avoid the bad without becoming a technologist? Follow this one simple rule:

> *Use technology to help you do what you should already be doing today. Avoid technology that tries to reinvent you.*

Beware of "Get Rich Fast" Technology Solutions

An example of technology to avoid at all costs is one that promises the "get rich fast" solution. Beware when the core benefit of a technology is to make you money (and a lot of it) in a revolutionary way that has never been done before. With real estate investing, the "get rich fast" schemes seem to be even more abundant. As your real estate investments grow, remember the fundamentals of what made you a successful investor. Don't be lured by the promise of reinventing you or your success. Instead, consider each technology purchase carefully, and look for solutions that repeat your success and make you more efficient.

A great lesson from history was the promise of the dot-com. The idea was simple: convert your business to an "e" business: eBanking, eRetail, eLearning, eShopping, eReal Estate, etc. Most companies that abandoned their past business models and success for the promise of the pure dot-com model were soon out of business.

Instead, the successful companies of the late 1990s captured the benefits and promises of this new technology. They used the Internet to help them do activities that they should have already been doing, such as communicate with customers or partners better, manage inventory more efficiently, or increase workforce productivity. When considering technology for your investment, choose and use solutions that make you better at what you should be already doing.

Important note: We all know of and hear about the Internet success stories such as Google, eBay, and Amazon. I would like to point out here that these companies used the Internet and technology to "invent" themselves, not "reinvent"—an important distinction.

Benefits of Online Internet Applications

The Internet has made possible a new type of software solution—the online Internet application. These solutions provide software functionality through a Web browser and Internet connection. You may already use some of these applications: Internet search (www.google.com), Web e-mail (www.hotmail.com), travel reservations (www.orbitz.com), or online banking. These types of applications are changing how we as consumers, businesses, and investors use computers. The benefits are tremendous:

1. No software to download or install—With an online application, the guts of the software reside on the host server, so you never have any software to download or install
2. Software updates are automatic—Online applications provide solutions with no maintenance for the end user. Software installed on your computer requires you to check for new software updates and fixes and perform regular maintenance. With your online solutions, maintenance is provided as part of the solution, and software updates materialize automatically to you
3. Access from any computer with an Internet connection—Because there is no software to install, you can access your online solution from any computer with a browser and Internet connectivity: you office, your home, your hotel's business center, or the library.
4. Data backup—With all of the computer viruses today, one of the biggest benefits of online solutions is the inherent data backup. Because your data resides on the host server, by default, you will not lose your data as a result of a hard drive crash or spilled cup of coffee.
5. Central security–As a general rule of thumb, it is easier for a single company to centralize and fortify its security defenses to protect and safeguard your data. An analogy is your bank; it has the collective resources and responsibility to protect your deposits. By letting your host online solution provider centralize the protection and security of your data, your data is like a deposit in the bank, securely guarded.

Let's look at a specific example: How can we use technology to better manage our real estate investment? Let's consider www.KeepMore.net, an online record-keeping solution.

- It will simplify your bookkeeping and administration—quickly capturing the funds going in (such as rent payments to you), and funds going out (such as building improvements) of your investment.
- It offers intelligent categorization—automatically sorting and categorizing your transactions so you know exactly how profitable you are during the year.

- It will simplify your tax time—Whether you use an accountant to file your returns or self-file, with one click, you can print reports and outline and summarize all the deductions and activity throughout the year.
- It will ensure that you maximize your investment potential—by leveraging all of the tax deduction techniques of this book and then recording the activity, tax time becomes a "pay day."
- It will continuously back up you data—With your data safely and securely backed up from you computer, you will never lose that crucial investment documentation.

Another example can be found in www.evaforhire.com (sponsor number 10297), where you can actually dictate tax, appointments, to-do's, and even e-mails and transfer this information from your dictating device to your computer to the Web automatically. Eva is a bit more expensive then KeepMore.net. Thus you might want to check out the features for both companies. You can find out more about both companies by going to Appendix 1, Recommended Tax Resources.

Using an online record-keeping solution allows you to leverage the power of the Internet, better protect your data, and use your time more efficiently. Most importantly, it does not attempt to reinvent you or the way that your real estate investment should work. It simply makes your life easier.

Understanding and Minimizing Internet Security Risks

"Security" once evoked images of gold and cash protected by armed guards and steel bars. On the Internet, information—not gold—is the precious resource. Locks and keys have given way to public key infrastructure, and steel bars to firewalls.

The Internet is beneficial because it lets you exchange data in seconds, but it also creates the risk of "spoofing." interception, and tampering. Understanding just a little bit about how Internet security works, may save you thousands of spam e-mails and maybe even protect you from a potential identity theft.

As a rule of thumb, when you do business on the Internet, use the same "street smarts" that you would have when doing business over the phone or at a retail shop. Throughout the month, we give our credit cards to cashiers or waiters, and we give out our account numbers over the phone when placing an order. It might surprise you to learn that it is actually safer, as long as we are using a trusted recipient, to pass confidential information over the Internet than in person or over the phone. That's because a trust Web site will help increase your "street smarts" and ensure that you are avoiding the two most common security dangers:

1. Impersonation: Is the person/business that takes my order authentic?
2. Eavesdropping: Could someone "listen in" to my order and steal my credit card information?

On the Internet today, we counter these security threats with a technology called SSL (Secure Sockets Layer). SSL is a set of rules followed by computers connected to the Internet. These rules include:

1. Encryption, which guards against eavesdropping
2. Data integrity, which assures that your communications aren't tampered with during transmission
3. Authentication, which verifies that the party actually receiving your communication is who it claims to be

It is easy for you to check a site's security status. Look at the site's URL (or Web address) in your browser window. An "s" added to the familiar "http" (to make "https") indicates that SSL is in effect. Most times, a valid SSL connection is represented by the symbol of a closed padlock on the bottom right of your Internet browser.

As technology progresses, you will need to continuously evaluate solutions for your real estate investment. Remember to follow one simple rule:

Use technology to help you do what you should already be doing today. Avoid technology that tries to reinvent you.

Appendix 3

Forms

Analyzing Your Rental Property Return on Investment

Tax Loss

Rental income	$
Commissions payable	$( )
Mortgage interest	$( )
Property taxes	$( )
Repairs	$( )
Property management	$( )
Insurance	$( )
Depreciation	$(_____)
Tax loss	$( )

Tax Refund

Tax loss	$
Tax rate	x _____
Tax refund	$ _____

Cash Flow

Rental income	$
Tax refund	$
Mortgage interest	$( )
Mortgage principal	$( )
Property taxes	$( )
Repairs	$( )
Property management	$( )
Insurance	$(_____)
Cash flow	$

Profit

Cash flow	$
Appreciation	$
Tax if sold	$(_____)
Net after-tax cash	$
Investment	÷$ _____
Net after-tax Return on investment	% _____

Tax Classification of Buyer's Settlement Statement Expenses

	TYPE OF PROPERTY	
	Investment	**Principal home**
Costs of obtaining title		
Real estate broker's commission	Basis	Basis
Finder's fees	Basis	Basis
Legal fees	Basis	Basis
Title search	Basis	Basis
Title policy charges	Basis	Basis
Title recording fees	Basis	Basis
Transfer (stamp) taxes	Basis	Basis
Survey	Basis	Basis
Costs incident to purchase		
Real estate taxes	Basis/Deduct	Basis/Deduct
Hazard insurance	Deduct	Nondeductible
Condominium fees	Deduct	Nondeductible
Utilities	Deduct	Nondeductible
Costs incident to loan		
Legal fees	Amortize	Nondeductible
Appraisal fees	Amortize	Nondeductible
Mortgage broker's commission	Amortize	Nondeductible
Pest inspection	Amortize	Nondeductible
Credit reports	Amortize	Nondeductible
Commitment fees	Amortize	Nondeductible
Loan fees (not points)	Amortize	Nondeductible
Mortgage insurance premiums	Deduct	Nondeductible
Costs representing prepayments of interest		
Points	Amortize	Deduct
Prepaid interest	Amortize	Deduct
VA and FHA points	Amortize	Deduct

Depreciation

Post-1986 Recovery Percentages
for Residential Rental Property (27.5 years)

Year	Month of Recovery Year											
	1	2	3	4	5	6	7	8	9	10	11	12
1	3.485	3.182	2.879	2.576	2.273	1.970	1.667	1.364	1.061	0.758	0.455	0.152
2–18	3.636	3.636	3.636	3.636	3.636	3.636	3.636	3.636	3.636	3.636	3.636	3.636
19–27	3.637	3.637	3.637	3.637	3.637	3.637	3.637	3.637	3.637	3.637	3.637	3.637
28	1.970	2.273	2.576	2.879	3.182	3.485	3.636	3.636	3.636	3.636	3.636	3.636
29	0.000	0.000	0.000	0.000	0.000	0.000	0.152	0.455	0.758	1.061	1.364	1.667

Post-May 23, 1993 Recovery Percentages
for Nonresidential Rental Property (40 years)

Year	Month of Recovery Year											
	1	2	3	4	5	6	7	8	9	10	11	12
1	2.461	2.247	2.033	1.819	1.605	1.391	1.177	0.963	0.749	0.535	0.321	0.107
2–39	2.564	2.564	2.564	2.564	2.564	2.564	2.564	2.564	2.564	2.564	2.564	2.564
40	0.107	0.321	0.535	0.749	0.963	1.177	1.391	1.605	1.189	2.033	2.247	2.461

Also see Figure 1-1 in Chapter 1.

Index

accountants and tax preparers, ix-x, 267-269
acquisition debt, interest payment deduction and, 40, 42
active participation, passive loss and, 112-113
allocation of tax basis, for depreciation, 121-122, 172
Alternative Minimum Tax (AMT), 5-6, 41-42, 57, 58, 92-93
   depreciation and, 92-93
   interest payment deduction and, 41-42
   real estate taxes and, 57, 58
appliances and fixtures
   improvements vs. repairs and, 34, 35
   record-keeping requirements of IRS and, 25
audits, xii, 107-121
authentication, online investing and, 217

basis. *See* tax basis, 19-23
bed-and-breakfast. *See* motels, hotels, B&Bs
bedroom rentals, interest payment deduction and, 42-43
Bracewell-Milnes, Barry, 95
Buffett, Warren, 109
building your home, tax deductions for, 51-53
Bush, George, 201
business use of vacation homes/second homes, 191

capital gain, 61. *See also* Universal Exclusion
   calculating, 153-154
   conversion of, 5
   depreciation and, 87
   like-kind exchange to avoid, 171-179
   community property states and, 75
   death and, 71-76, 71
   depreciation and, 90
   divorce and, 62-63, 65, 71-76
   Home Handy-Man Relief Act and, 63-64
   Home Sale Exclusion and, 22
   Itinerant Landlord Relief Act and, 64
   S corporations and, 77-81
   sales to relatives and, 181-183
   Universal Exclusion and, 61-66, 67-70
cash vs. like-kind exchange, 175, 178
charitable donation of use of vacation homes/second homes, 191-192, 193
children
   hiring of, for income splitting, 136-138
   Kiddie Tax and, 130-131

clearing and grading costs, depreciation and, 122, 124-125
Clinton, Bill, 201
closely held corporations, 117
closing costs (settlement)
   form for calculating, 220
   nondeductible items and, 29
   record-keeping requirements of IRS and, 25, 27-28, 27
community property states, capital gains and, 75
construction loans, 51-53
conversion, taxes and, 5
corporations
   Limited Liability Companies (LLC) and, 202
   rules for, by state, 211
   types of, 202-203
   C corporations
      closely held, 117
      passive loss and, 117
   S corporation
      Universal Exclusion and, 77-81
cost of looking for rental property, as deduction, 101-106, 105
   for first property, 101-102
   for "rental businesses", 103-104, 103
   targeted purchase acquisition and, 104
   targeted purchase failure and, 102-103

data integrity, online investing and, 217
death and taxes, 71-76
   estate taxes and, 23
   tax basis and, 22
   Universal Exclusion and, 71-76
deductions, 4
   Alternative Minimum Tax (AMT) and, 5-6, 41-42, 57, 58, 92-93
   building your home and, 51-53
   construction loans and, 51-53
   cost of looking for property as, 101-106, 105
   depreciation and, 89-93, 121-125
   "home" defined for, 39-40
   improvements vs. repairs and, 31-36
   income splitting and, 127-134
   itemized, 7-8, 55-58. *See also* itemized deductions
   land costs as, 127-134
   land interest payments and, 52
   mortgage interest and, 4, 37-43
   points on mortgage and, 45-49
   qualified home defined for, 38-39, 42

deductions *(Continued)*
real estate taxes and, 55-58
special assessments and, 57, 58
tax basis and, 7-9
transfer and recording fees and, 57, 58
deferrals, tax, 5
deferred like-kind exchange, 175, 178
demolition costs, 123-124, 125
depreciation, 89-93, 121-125
allocation of tax basis for, 121-122
Alternative Minimum Tax (AMT) and, 92-93
calculating, 89, 91-92, 91, 221
capital gain and, 90
clearing and grading costs in, 122, 124-125
landscaping and, 123
like-kind exchange and, recapture of, 172
maximizing deductions for, 121-125
motels, hotels, B&Bs and, 197, 199
preparing land for building, demolition costs and,
123-124, 133
recapture of, 165, 172
record-keeping requirements of IRS and, 25
rental properties and, 95
residential vs. commercial real estate and, 91-92, 91
seller financing (installment sales) and, recapture
and, 165
tax basis and, 19, 25
Universal Exclusion and, recapture of, 63, 65
when to start, 90-91
divorce and taxes, 71-76
community property states and, 75
Universal Exclusion and, 62-63, 65, 71-76
dwelling unit defined, 189-190, 193

eavesdropping, online investing and, 217
economics and real estate, 13-14
EDayTraderTax.com, 210
employment contracts when hiring relatives, 139
encryption, online investing and, 217
escrow accounts
like-kind exchange and, interest earnings on, 177
seller financing (installment sales) and, 161-162, 168
estate taxes, 23
estimated tax payments, 8
EvaforHire.com, 210, 216
excess mortgage trap, with seller financing
(installment sales), 163-165, 168
exclusions, tax, 4
Home Sale Exclusion and, 22
Universal Exclusion and, 4, 59, 61-66. *See also*
Universal Exclusion
exercise price, option, 205

Fairey vs. Commissioners, 103
Farmer's Creamery case, defining improvements
vs. repairs, 146
Financial and Tax Fraud Education Associates, 211
financing your purchase. *See also* mortgages; seller
financing
construction loans and, 51-53
interest rates and, 14, 16
leverage and, 12-13
mortgage insurance and, 15-16
mortgages and, 37-43
nondeductible closing costs and, 29
points and, 45-49
seller financing in. *See* seller financing
Fincalc.com, 211

forms, 219-221
frequently asked questions, 201-207
"get rich fast" technology solutions, 214
gift-leaseback technique, 131-132
gifted property
gift-leaseback technique in, 131-132
to relatives, income splitting strategy using, 128-131
tax basis and, 20-21, 23
Godfrey, Arthur, 31
grantor/grantee, options, 205
Guttman, G., 127

H and R Block, 210
hardship exception for two-year rule, Universal
Exclusion and, 68-69
hiring children, 136-138
hiring spouses, income splitting and, 135
home equity debt, interest payment deduction and, 40-41
Home Handy-Man Relief Act, Universal Exclusion
and, 63-64
home ownership, 3-10, 11-16
Alternative Minimum Tax (AMT) and, 5-6, 41-42,
57, 58, 92-93
building your home and, tax deductions for, 51-53
capital gain and, 5
conversion and, 5
depreciation and, 91-92, 91
estimated tax payments and, 8
Home Sale Exclusion and, 22
improvements vs. repairs and, 31-36, 142
itemized deductions and, 7-8
leverage and, 12-13
mortgage payments and, 4
passive losses and, 5
real estate taxes and, 55-58
renting vs., 6-9, 11
S corporations and, 77-81
tax basis and, 19-23
tax deductions and, 4, 7-9
tax deferral and, 5
tax exclusions and, 4
tax planning concepts for, 4-5
Universal Exclusion and, 4, 59, 61-66
vacation home limitations and, 5, 187-194.
See also vacation homes/second homes
withholding allowance and, 7-9
Home Sale Exclusion, 22
"home" defined, 39-40
Hoover, Herbert, 37
hotels. *See* motels, hotels, B&Bs
hybrid debt, interest payment deduction and, 41-42

icons used in book, xiii
impersonation, online investing and, 217
improvements vs. repairs, 31-36, 141-150
appliances, fixtures and, 34, 35
bulletproof repair strategies for, 145-146
defining, 142
documentation of, as proof, 144-145
examples of disputed cases of, 147-148
Farmer's Creamery case in, defining, 146
gray area of definition for, 142-143
in homes and principal residences, 142
Jacobson case in, defining, 143-144
landscaping and, 34, 35
record-keeping requirements of IRS and, 25, 147
in rental properties, 95
special assessments and, 33

improvements vs. repairs *(Continued)*
  tests for, 32-33
  in timeshares, 202
  in vacation homes/second homes, 190, 193
income splitting, 127-134, 135-139
  gift-leaseback technique in, 131-132
  gifting property to relatives as, 128-131
  hiring children for, 136-138
  hiring relatives for, documentation strategies for, 138
  hiring spouses for, 135
  Kiddie Tax and, 130-131
  selling and leasing back technique for, 132-133
inherited property, tax basis and, 21-22, 23
installment sales. *See* seller financing (installment sales)
insurance
  on mortgage, 15-16
  for rental properties and, 95
interest earnings
  like-kind exchange and, escrow amounts, 177
  seller financing (installment sales) and, 157-158, 162, 167
interest payment deduction (mortgage), 37-43
  acquisition debt and, 40, 42
  Alternative Minimum Tax (AMT) and, 41-42
  bedroom rentals and, 42-43
  building your home and, 51-53
  construction loans and, 51-53
  home equity debt and, 40-41
  "home" defined for, 39-40
  hybrid debt and, 41-42
  land and, 52
  phaseout of, 58
  qualified home defined for, 38-39, 42
interest rates, 14, 16
Internal Revenue Code (IRC), 1
Internet security risks, online investing and, 216-217
Intuit, 210
IRAs and real estate investment, 203-204
IRS Regulations (REGS), 1
IRS.gov, 210
itemized deductions, 7-8
  phaseout of, 58
  real estate taxes and, 55-58
Itinerant Landlord Relief Act, 64

Jacobson case in, defining improvement vs. repair, 143-144
joint ownership, 203
  tax basis and, 22

KeepMore.net, 216
Keynes, John Maynard, 195
Kiddie Tax, 130-131
Kiplinger's, 211

land purchases
  allocation of tax basis and, 121-122, 172
  clearing and grading costs in, 122, 124-125
  deductions associated with, 127-134
  gifting property to relatives, income splitting strategy using, 128-131
  income splitting and, 127-134
  interest payment deductions and, 52
  preparing land for building, demolition costs and, 123-124, 125
landscaping
  depreciation and, 123
  improvements vs. repairs and, 34, 35
  record-keeping requirements of IRS and, 25
  Twenty Feet Rule for, 34

Laughlinusa.com, 211
leasing
  gift-leaseback technique in, 131-132
  selling and leasing back technique for, 132-133
leverage, 12-13
like-kind exchange, 171-179
  allocation of land/building basis and, 172
  benefits of, 172
  cash and, 175, 178
  deferred, 175, 178
  depreciation recapture and, 172
  disqualified persons as intermediaries in, 174, 177, 178
  interest earnings of escrow amounts and, 177
  intermediaries in, 173-174, 177, 178
  location of properties in, 176
  mortgage relief using, 175-176
  overview of process of, 172-173
  principal residences and, 173
  relatives and, 177
  replacement properties in, naming of, 177
  rules applicable to, 176-177
  tax avoidance on, 175
  tax basis and, 172
  types of, 173
Limited Liability Companies (LLC), 202
loss
  calculating, 153-154
  depreciation and, 87
  motels, hotels, B&Bs and, 197, 199, 197
  passive, 5, 165-166
  rental properties, 96, 97-98, 109-119
    passive loss and, 109-119, 109
  sales to relatives and, 181-183
  seller financing (installment sales) and, 165-166
  vacation homes/second homes and, disallowed, 188, 193
Lower Your Taxes Big Time, 45, 135, 195, 203, 209

management fees, 14-15, 16, 96
material participation, passive loss and, 115-117
mental incapacity exception for two-year rule, Universal Exclusion and, 69, 70
Millionaire Next Door, The, x
minors. *See* children
Money Management, 211
Money Mastery, x, 11, 211
Monster.com, 210
mortgage insurance, 15-16
mortgages, 37-43
  acquisition debt and, 40, 42
  home equity debt and, 40-41
  hybrid debt and, 41-42
  interest payment deductions and, 4, 37-43
  like-kind exchange and, 175-176
  mortgage insurance and, 15-16
  points on, 45-49
  refinancing and, hybrid debt, 41-42
  rental properties and, 95, 96
  seller financing (installment sales) and, excess mortgage trap of, 163-165, 168
motels, hotels, B&Bs, 195-200
  defining a hotel for, 198, 199
  depreciation for, 197, 199
  downsides of, 197-198
  income reporting for, IRS compliance with, 196-197, 199
  loss reporting for, Schedule C, 197, 199
  personal use of, 198, 199
  rates charged by, documentation of, 197, 199
  Social Security taxes and, 198, 199

motels, hotels, B&Bs *(Continued)*
  tax advantages of, 197, 199
  travel rules and, 195-196, 199
  worker rules for, 199
myths of tax planning, ix-xi

nondeductible items, closing and settlement, 29

online Internet real estate investment applications, 215
option trading on real estate, tax consequences of, 205-207
origination fees (VA/FHA loans), 47
other people's money (OPM), 12
ownership, types of, 202-203

passive activity losses (PAL), 110. *See also* passive loss
passive income generators (PIGs) in, 110.
  See also passive loss
passive loss, 5, 109-119
  active participation defined in, 112-113
  corporate exceptions to limits in, 117
  limitations to, exceptions to, 111-114
  loss deduction for rental property and, 112-113
  material participation defined for, 115-117
  passive activity defined for, 110, 110
  passive activity losses (PAL) in, 110
  passive income generators (PIGs) in, 110
  real estate professionals and, 114-115, 201-202
  sale of passive property and, 111-112
  seller financing (installment sales) and, 165-166
  suspension (and carryover of), 110-111
pension plans and real estate investment, 203-204
performance bonds, building your home and, 52, 53
points on mortgage, 45-49
  seller-paid, 47
  tax planning strategy for, 48
  VA and FHA origination fees and, 47
premium, option, 205
preparing land for building, 123-124, 125
principal residences, like-kind exchange and, 173
prorating, real estate taxes and, 56-58
purchased property, tax basis of, 20, 23

qualified home, interest payment deduction and, 38-39, 42
QuatLoos.com, 211

rate of return, rental properties, 95-99
Reagan, Ronald, 25
real estate professionals, passive loss and, 114-115, 201-202
real estate taxes, 55-58
  allocations in year of sale for, 55-56, 58
  Alternative Minimum Tax (AMT) and, 57, 58
  phaseout of deduction for, 58
  prorating and, 56-57, 58
  rental properties and, 95
  special assessments and, 57, 58
  transfer and recording fees and, 57, 58
recapture of depreciation, 165, 172
record-keeping requirements of IRS, 25-30
  appliances, fixtures and, 25
  closing costs and, 25, 27-28, 27
  depreciation and, 25
  employment contracts when hiring relatives and, 139
  hiring relatives and, 138
  improvements vs. repairs and, 25, 147
  landscaping and, 25
  nondeductible items and, 29
  records to keep in, 26-27

record-keeping requirements of IRS *(Continued)*
  technology/software for, 213
  time to keep records in, 26
refinancing a mortgage, hybrid debt and, 41-42
refunds, tax, 7
relatives
  capital gain vs. losses in sales to, 181-183
  defined, for tax purposes, 182-183
  documentation of employment for, 138
  employment contracts when hiring relatives and, 139
  like-kind exchange and, 177
  sales to, 181-183
  seller financing (installment sales) and, 162-163, 168
  Universal Exclusion and, 79-80, 81
"rental businesses" defined, 103-104
rental properties, 85-88
  bedroom rentals as, in your own home, 42-43
  capital gain and, 87
  cost of looking for, 101-106, 105
  depreciation and, 89-93, 95, 121-125
  improvements vs. repairs in, 95, 142-150
  income from, 95
  insurance costs of, 95
  introduction to, 85-88
  loss and, 87, 96, 97-98, 109-119
  management fees and, 96
  mortgage payments on, 95, 96
  passive loss and, 109-119
  rate of return calculation for, 95-99
  real estate taxes and, 95
  S corporations and, 77-81
  selling, taxes on, 96
  tax basis and, 86
  Universal Exclusion and, 64, 80, 81
  vacancy rate for, 96
  vacation homes/second homes and, tax free rent income from, 190, 193
renting vs. home ownership, 6-9, 11
repairs. *See* improvements vs. repairs
repossession, seller financing (installment sales) and, 159-160, 167
retirement planning and real estate investment, 203-204
return on investment, 1
  form for, 219
Rostenkowski, Dan, 101

S corporations and Universal Exclusion, 77-81
Sagefire International, 210
sales to relatives, 181-183
school location and real estate value, 15, 16
Secure Sockets Layer (SSL), 217
seller financing (installment sales), 155-169
  advantages of, 157-160, 167
  default by buyer and, structuring the deal for maximum profits in, 158-159
  depreciation recapture and, 165
  electing out of installment reporting in, 166, 167
  escrow accounts and, 161-162, 168
  excess mortgage trap caused by, 163-165, 168
  installment sales in, 155-156
  interest earnings and, 157-158, 162, 167
  passive losses and, 165-166
  problem potentials with, 162-165
  /to relatives, 162-163, 168
  repossession profits using, 159-160, 167
  seller take-backs and, 160
  tax payments lowered by, 158
  Universal Exclusion and, 168

selling and leasing back technique, income splitting, 132-133
selling rental properties, 96
separation. *See* divorce and taxes
settlement. *See* closing costs
Shaw, George Bernard, 121
Social Security taxes, motels, hotels, B&Bs and, 198, 199
software, tax preparation, 204-205
special assessments, real estate taxes and, 57, 58
swaps and barters, vacation homes/second homes and, 192, 193

Tax Advisor magazine, 210
tax basis, 19-23
    allocation of land/building in, 121-122, 172
    depreciation and, 19, 25, 86
    gain/loss calculation using, 154
    gifted property and, 20-21, 23
    improvements vs. repairs and, 31-36
    inherited property and, 21-22, 23
    joint property and, 22
    like-kind exchange and, 172
    overall formula for, 35
    purchased property and, 20, 23
    record-keeping requirements of IRS and, 25-30
    special assessments and, 33
tax code, 1
tax planning, ix-xi
tax preparation, ix-x, 210
tax preparation software, 204-205
Tax Strategies for Business Professionals, 195
taxes
    Alternative Minimum Tax (AMT) and, 5-6, 41-42, 57, 58, 92-93
    capital gain and. *See* capital gains
    children and, 136-138
    conversion and, 5
    death and. *See* death and taxes
    deductions and. *See* deductions
    deferrals of, 5
    depreciation. *See* depreciation
    divorce and. *See* divorce and taxes
    estate taxes and, 23
    estimated payments of, 8
    exclusions from, 4
    Home Sale Exclusion and, 22
    improvements vs. repairs and, deductions to, 31-36
    itemized deductions and, 7-8
    Kiddie Tax and, 130-131
    like-kind exchange to avoid, 171-179
    option trading on real estate, 205-207
    passive loss and, 5, 109-119
    real estate taxes and, 55-58
    recommended resources for, 209-211
    record-keeping requirements of IRS and, 25-30
    refunds on, 7
    rental properties and, upon sale of, 96
    seller financing (installment sales) and, 158
    tax basis and, 19-23. *See also* tax basis
    Universal Exclusion and. *See* Universal Exclusion
    vacation home limitations and, 5, 187-194.
        See also vacation homes/second homes
    withholding allowance and, 7-9
TaxReductionInstitute.com, 209
TaxSites.com, 210
TaxWorld.org, 210

technology and real estate investment, 213-217
    "get rich fast" solutions and, 214
    Internet security risks and, 216-217
    online Internet applications using, 215-216
    pros and cons of, 213-214
tenant by entirety, 203
tenants in common, 203
timeshares, 192-193, 202
TradersAccounting.com, 210
transfer and recording fees, 57, 58
travel rules, motels, hotels, B&Bs and, 195-196, 199
TurboTax.com, 210
Twenty Feet Rule for landscaping, 34
Two-Out-of-Five-Year requirement, Universal Exclusion and, 62, 65

unemployment rates and real estate value, 15, 16
unforeseen circumstances exception for two-year rule, Universal Exclusion and, 69, 70
Universal Exclusion, 4, 59, 61-66, 67-70
    death and, 71-76
    depreciation and, recapture of, 63, 65
    divorce and, 62-63, 65, 71-76
    electing out of, 64-65
    exceptions to two-year rule for, 67-70
    hardship exception for two-year rule and, 68-69
    Home Handy-Man Relief Act and, 63-64
    Itinerant Landlord Relief Act and, 64
    joint filers not sharing a residence and, 62-63, 65
    mental incapacity exception for two-year rule and, 69, 70
    rental properties and, moving into, 80, 81
    S corporations and, 77-81
    sale to relatives and, meeting the two-year rule with, 79-80, 81
    seller financing (installment sales) and, 168
    Two-Out-of-Five-Year requirement in, 62, 65
    unforeseen circumstances exception for two-year rule and, 69, 70
    use of, once every two years rule for, 63, 65, 67-70

VA and FHA origination fees, points on mortgage and, 47
vacancy rate, rental properties and, 96
vacation homes/second homes, 187-194
    business use of, 191
    charitable donation of use of, 191-192, 193
    dwelling unit defined for, 189-190, 193
    increases to personal use, avoiding, 192, 193
    limitations to tax benefits of, 5, 187-194
    losses and, disallowed, 188, 193
    minimums of personal use for, 188-189,193
    repairs to, 190, 193
    swaps and barters of, 192, 193
    tax free rent from, 190, 193
    timeshares in, 192-193, 202
valuation of real estate, 15, 16

Walton, Sam, x
websites of interest, tax resources, 209-211
Williams, Alan, 11, 211
withholding allowance, 7-9